Edward S Ellis

Across Texas

Edward S Ellis

Across Texas

ISBN/EAN: 9783744693073

Printed in Europe, USA, Canada, Australia, Japan

Cover: Foto ©Andreas Hilbeck / pixelio.de

More available books at **www.hansebooks.com**

THE TARANTULA. *Page 52.*

"Forest and Fire" Series of Books for Boys

ACROSS TEXAS

BY

EDWARD S. ELLIS

Author of "The Cabin in the Clearing,"
&c. &c.

T. NELSON AND SONS
London, Edinburgh, and New York

1894

CONTENTS.

I.	A LETTER AND A TELEGRAM,	....	1
II.	THROUGH TO TEXAS,	....	10
III.	IN SAN ANTONIO, ...	....	20
IV.	A STARTLING INTERRUPTION,	....	29
V.	A TEST OF ONE'S NERVES,	....	38
VI.	TWO GOOD SHOTS, ...	....	49
VII.	AN INTRUDER IN CAMP,	....	59
VIII.	BELL RICKARD, ...	....	69
IX.	DEPARTURE OF THE GUEST,	....	78
X.	DANGER IN THE EAST,	....	87
XI.	STRANGE PROCEEDINGS,	....	96
XII.	WHAT DOES IT MEAN?	....	105
XIII.	AN UNEXPECTED SIGNAL,	....	114
XIV.	A STRANGE ABSENCE, ...	....	123
XV.	CAUGHT FOUL, ...	....	132
XVI.	AN ASTOUNDING DISCOVERY,	....	141
XVII.	THE SOLITARY PURSUER,	....	150
XVIII.	THE SECOND RANGE OF HILLS, ...	....	159
XIX.	IN THE RAVINE, ...	....	168

XX. REINFORCEMENTS,	....	176
XXI. THE PURSUIT,	....	186
XXII. ACROSS THE BORDER,	....	195
XXIII. A RELIC OF OTHER DAYS,	....	204
XXIV. A RACE WITH AN AVALANCHE,	....	213
XXV. THE RANCH,	....	222
XXVI. BELL RICKARD'S SCHEME,	....	230
XXVII. WATCHING AND WAITING,	....	239
XXVIII. THE SOUND OF A PISTOL,	....	248
XXIX. THROUGH THE NIGHT,	....	257
XXX. A FIGURE IN THE DARKNESS,	....	266
XXXI. THE RETURN,	....	275
XXXII. THE ENCOUNTER,	....	284
XXXIII. IMPORTANT NEGOTIATIONS,	....	291
XXXIV. A STRANGE DISCOVERY,	....	302
XXXV. THROUGH THE LINES AGAIN,	....	311
XXXVI. THE DECISION,	....	320
XXXVII. THE FINAL CHARGE,	....	329
XXXVIII. CONCLUSION,	....	337

ACROSS TEXAS.

CHAPTER I.

A LETTER AND A TELEGRAM.

NICK RIBSAM, of whom I had considerable to tell you in "The Young Moose Hunters," returned to his humble home in Western Pennsylvania with his health fully restored by his stirring experience in the mountainous forests of Maine. He was naturally strong and active, and one glance at his bright eyes, his ruddy cheeks, and his alert movements told his sister Nellie and the beloved father and mother that the prescription of the physician had worked like a charm.

Nick was now a sturdy youth, a bright scholar and a general favorite with all who knew him. His parents were not of the kind that are demonstrative, but their hearts were wrapped up in their worthy son, and they were full of gratitude that he should come back to them at the end of what, after all, was only a brief absence, without a trace of the weakness that caused them so much misgiving when he went away.

They felt a strong friendship and affection, too, for Herbert Watrous and his parents, through whose kindness the trip down East was brought about. There was no "discounting" the fondness of the Watrouses for the manly youth. Mr. Watrous, as has been shown, possessed large means, and denied his son nothing, his affection for Herbert leading him astray in that respect. But he saw the great good done his boy through his association with Nick. You know that the most forceful sermon ever preached is that of example. It matters little what a person says, but it is everything what he does. It is not the profession, but the life which must be the test, as it certainly will be before the final Judge of all mankind.

Mr. Watrous and his wife welcomed Herbert home, and their eyes sparkled at sight of the immense stuffed moose forming a striking trophy of the young man's visit to Uncle Dick Musgrove. He could not be blamed for feeling proud over his prize, and for having a number of large photographs struck off and sent to his friends, but that which touched the parents' hearts was the change in Herbert himself. He had always been fond of them, but with that feeling was now mingled a tender respect that had been wanting before. He never forgot their wishes; he showed a deeper interest in his studies; he abandoned habits and associations which he knew his parents disliked; he made a confidant of his father as well as his mother, and consulted with them and asked their counsel in whatever important step he had in mind.

Now, what had wrought this change in Herbert Watrous? Nick had done very little "preaching" to him. True, whenever the chance was inviting, he dropped a word or two that clinched an important principle, and now and then, when their long talks took a favorable drift, he gave his views with a power and point that could not be mistaken, but it was the daily life of Nick that did the blessed work.

A family holding the social position of Mr. Watrous in New York has no lack of privileges for a son; but there was nothing that gave Herbert the genuine pleasure that he gained by a visit to Nick Ribsam, in his quiet country home in Western Pennsylvania. The pure air, the healthful food, the perfect cooking, the cleanliness that was everywhere, the cheerfulness, the mutual love and confidence, the warm welcome from everyone — these brought to him an enjoyment and satisfaction far beyond what mere wealth can buy.

It was during the early autumn succeeding the incidents told in "The Moose Hunters," that Herbert paid his second visit to Nick. The latter met him at the railway station, but the delight of welcoming his old friend to his country home was sadly marred by the appearance of Herbert. Beyond a doubt he was in a bad way. He was nearly six feet tall, very slim, with a flushed face, a dragging walk, short breath, and, indeed, with every sign of incipient consumption.

"I know what you are thinking about," said he, with a wan smile, "but I don't look any worse than I feel."

"You do look bad," replied Nick, as he drove homeward in their old-fashioned carriage. "What does it mean?"

"I hardly know; the doctor says I am growing too fast, have studied too hard, and haven't had enough exercise. You know I meant to enter Yale this fall and have been boning like the mischief. But I have given up that and postponed college for a year at least, and," he added with a sigh, "perhaps forever."

"You mustn't talk that way," said Nick, pained beyond expression; "you must stop all study and live outdoors for a few weeks. You have no bad habits, Herbert?"

"None at all, though I may be reaping the penalty of my former foolishness; but I haven't touched tobacco or alcohol in any form for six months."

"I see no reason why you should not come out all right in a short time," added Nick, uttering the wish rather than the belief he felt.

"I have a letter in my pocket from my father to your father; I know what is in it, but I will let him tell you himself."

Home being reached, the team put away, and a kind welcome given to Herbert by Nellie and her parents, all sat down to the meal awaiting them. At its conclusion, Herbert handed the letter he bore to Mr. Ribsam, who curiously broke the seal.

When he saw it was written in English he smiled and passed it to his son.

"I vill lets Nick read him, cause I don't English reads as vell as German as I don't."

Nick took the missive and read aloud, the others listening attentively:

"New York, October 13, 18—
"My Dear Mr. Ribsam:

"My son Herbert has expressed the gratitude which his mother and myself will ever feel toward your noble son Nicholas, for the immeasurable good he has done my boy by his precept and example. That influence will follow him like a blessing through life, and you and your good wife are to be congratulated on having such a worthy child.

"I am about to ask a great favor of you. We are alarmed for Herbert's health. It is certainly singular that last winter it was your son whose condition was bad, while now it is my own who is in a condition that causes us the gravest alarm. I have consulted the best physicians in New York, who tell me that he is threatened with consumption; that medicine will not cure him, but, like your own son last year, he must give up his indoors life at home and secure a radical change of air and surroundings.

"I would arrange to have him spend a few weeks with you, where I know he is welcome, but the medical men tell me that he runs a risk so long as he is exposed to a northern climate, with its sudden and violent changes.

"We have considered the question of a sea voyage, and a winter in the Bermudas, the West Indies, or in Southern France; but there are objections to all these, the principal of which is our dislike to have him go out of our own country, where he would have to meet a new language, different kinds of people, and unfavorable surroundings.

"The plan we have decided upon is to send him on a tour through the southwestern section of our own country. We have arranged for him to visit Texas, Arizona, New Mexico, and Southern California, hoping that by the return of spring he will be so fully restored to health that he can come home as sound in body as your own son.

"The favor I ask of you is that you will consent that Nicholas shall accompany him. I am aware that this is asking a great sacrifice of you, and I have hesitated a long time before putting the request on paper. You need your boy at home with you; it will cause you and his mother and sisters great misgiving to let him go away for five or six months, and no doubt involve considerable pecuniary loss. Still, my solicitude for my own child forces me to ask this great sacrifice at your hands.

"In doing so, there are several conditions upon which I shall insist. The first is that under no circumstances shall it cost you or your son a penny. My position in railway matters enables me to secure, without trouble, passes on the leading lines from your home over the entire route and return. These passes are now in Herbert's possession. Other expenses will be involved, as some of the travelling will have to be done in stage coaches and on horseback, to say nothing of the cost of living. All this is provided for. My son has letters to bankers at various points *en route* which will secure him ample funds. They will need no outfit until they reach San Antonio, and start further westward. It is my earnest wish that if Nicholas accompanies Herbert, doing so as his friend, companion, and, in one sense, his escort, I shall be permitted to make compensation therefor, as properly due you for loss of his valuable services.

"If you will consent that your son shall go with him, I advise that the start be made at once from your house. If you feel that I am presuming too much on your kindness do not hesitate to say so, and I will try to make other arrangements.

"I am, my dear sir, very truly yours,
"J. H. WATROUS."

To quote a familiar expression, the reading of this letter produced a sensation. Every eye was fixed on Nick, as he sat in his chair with the missive in his hand, and pronounced the words in a clear voice.

It is not necessary to give the conversation that followed, for it was a long one in which all shared, but late that afternoon Nick harnessed up the old roan again and drove to the railway station with Herbert. Hastily leaving the vehicle, they passed into the telegraph office, where the city youth wrote out a telegram addressed to his father, and it ran thus:

It is all fixed : Nick and I leave for Texas and the southwest to-morrow. Good-by, and love to you and mother.
HERBERT.

CHAPTER II.

THROUGH TO TEXAS.

LET me skip a great deal of what may be called introduction, for of necessity it bore a resemblance to that which has already been told, and has little if any connection with the main events of my story.

Mr. Watrous' arrangements for the comfort of the boys was perfect. The ride to St. Louis in the famous Limited Express was the luxury of railway travelling, and they landed in the Mound City within twenty-four hours after leaving Philadelphia, where Nick met his old friend, Ned Osmun, who had given to him his wonderful ride on his engine to Jersey City. He wished them every pleasure on their long journey, which he said caused him a touch of envy, but he meant to even-up matters by another fishing excursion in Western Pennsylvania, with a call on Nick's parents and pretty Nellie.

They stayed overnight at the Lindell in St. Louis, but were in such a hurry to reach their destination that, without spending any time in visiting the sights and interesting scenes, they left the following morning over the Iron Mountain Railway for Texarkana.

This ride, though long and at times tedious, was enjoyed by both, for the scenes and incidents gave a foretaste of what was coming. A number of cattlemen were on the train, and the boys struck up an acquaintance with them. They found them pleasant and ready to impart all the information that was asked for.

There were long hours of riding through the dismal pine woods of Missouri and Arkansas, where, mile after mile, they saw only an occasional settler's cabin, with the half-dressed children playing around the door. In several cases, the openings between the logs were so large that they could look through both the front and rear of the structure and see the trees on the other side.

They left the train at Malvern, and took the narrow gauge railway to the celebrated Hot

Springs, twenty-five miles distant, where they stayed overnight. One of the interesting facts learned here was the clever manner in which "Diamond Jo," who built and owns the narrow gauge railway, outwitted the Arkansas Legislature, which forbade a charge of more than five cents a mile on every line in the State between any two places. The capitalist named had been charging and receiving ten cents a mile, and he now flanked the law by locating the western terminus of his line within two or three feet of the boundary of Hot Springs, and continued serenely to receive his excessive rates as before.

They reached Texarkana Saturday evening, and, since there was no travelling westward on Sunday, that day was spent in the town, which lies partly within Texas and partly within Arkansas, and includes within its odd name a portion of the appellation of each of the two States.

They attended church, which was capable of accommodating fifty people by crowding, and whose walls contained but a single placard, which was a request for the attendants not to spit on the floor.

The next stopping place was at Austin, the capital of Texas. The weather was quite warm, but the nights were cool and breezy, and the glimpses of the snowy cotton fields were a treat to the boys, who looked upon them for the first time.

They spent one night and a portion of a day in Austin, visiting the capitol and strolling through the city, which contains many fine buildings of white marble-like stone, peculiar to the vicinity. In the capitol they saw several fine paintings of the early heroes of Texas. On the cenotaph (since destroyed by the burning of the capitol), was the inscription to the memory of the defenders of the Alamo, which is one of the most striking tributes ever conceived by man: "THERMOPYLÆ HAD ITS MESSENGER OF DEFEAT: THE ALAMO HAD NONE."

The railway line to San Antonio had recently been finished, and they arrived in that quaint old town as night was closing in. A bright moon was shining in an unclouded sky, and, after registering at the Menger House, facing the Plaza, they strolled through the city and enjoyed a view of the Alamo by moonlight.

The brown adobe walls were softened in the mild radiance, and, as Nick described the defence made by the garrison of less than two hundred men against four thousand Mexicans under Santa Anna, it seemed to Herbert that he was witnessing that tremendous fight, which continued for eleven days, until only a dozen grimy, panting, and exhausted defenders were left. The terrible Colonel Bowie was shot in his sick bed, and Davy Crockett was among the handful that at last surrendered, under the promise of honorable treatment, but were treacherously massacred by Santa Anna.

The winding Colorado was impressively beautiful in the moonlight, and the adobe mission houses, which were visited the next day, were viewed with the interest that all tourists feel when they first look upon them. Each was over a century old. One, in a fine state of preservation, was pointed out, where the Jesuit fathers were besieged by the Comanche Indians for nearly two years.

Among the curiosities noticed in San Antonio were the Mexican dogs, without a hair on their bodies, and the other canines, known as "tramps" or "nobody's dogs," who roam over the country between the city and the Rio Grande, picking up their food, as do their biped brothers, and confessing to the ownership of no one. That portion of San Antonio called Mexico was squalid, and made up of old residents, many of whom cannot speak a word of English, while in other sections nearly everyone understands English, Spanish, and German.

The boys stayed several days in this city, for they looked upon it as their real starting point or entrance into the great southwest. They had talked over the question while on their way thither, and agreed upon the line to be followed. Herbert had a letter of recommendation to Mr. Lord, a banker, by which he could secure all the funds needed, and who showed a wish to help him in every way in his power.

He invited the boys to visit him at his house, where they spent an evening with the gentleman, who, having been a resident in Texas from a date several years before the Civil

War, was able to give the very knowledge and counsel they needed. He told them a fact that they had not noticed. San Antonio itself is a resort for invalids threatened with, or suffering from, pulmonary weakness, who find the mild, equable climate very helpful. He had known of cases in which it had wrought a complete cure.

"But I see," he said with a smile, "that that doesn't suit your ideas; while there are many sights here that you have not seen—such as the Colorado Springs—yet you could not content yourselves in our sleepy town for more than a day or two longer. You can take the stage from here to El Paso, but the ride is tiresome, and, at this season of the year, dusty and trying to a degree."

"I don't think we should fancy that," said Nick, who refrained from giving a hint of the plan they had formed.

"I suppose you are both good horsemen?" was the inquiring remark of the banker.

They answered that they were fairly good riders. Nick had learned to ride horses almost as soon as he could walk, and Herbert had taken instructions at an academy in New York for a couple of years past.

"Everybody rides a horse or burro in Texas," said Mr. Lord, "and the only caution you need is to make sure you possess a clear title to the animal you throw your leg over. There are few people hanged in Texas for murder, but plenty are strung up every year for horse-stealing. You would be objects of suspicion if you should take a walk out in the country. My advice, then, is to buy three excellent ponies, provide yourselves with a good outfit, including a fine repeating Winchester rifle and a revolver apiece, with plenty of ammunition. You will need an extra animal to carry your luggage. Then strike out for New Mexico. You will have to ride a clean five hundred miles before crossing the boundary, but it is the right season of the year, and the ride will do you good."

"Do you advise us to go alone?" asked Herbert.

"By no means; you must have companions who are familiar with the country, and they can be easily secured."

"How?"

"There are hunters, miners, prospectors, and adventurers in San Antonio all the time, who have either just come from the wild regions beyond or are about to set out for them. They may be rough in their ways, but they are generally honest and trustworthy, and there will be no trouble in engaging them as companions."

"You have laid out the plan Herbert and I had fixed upon, but we felt doubts about being able to carry it out. We have informed ourselves, so far as we can, concerning the country over which we wish to ride, and the more we learned, the more we saw the need of having men who were familiar with it. How about the Indians?"

"Well, you are liable to meet them, but I do not think there is much to be feared, as I have heard no disquieting rumors lately, though," added the banker significantly, "I was shot at myself, within the present year, by a party of marauding Comanches, within six miles of San Antonio. When you get into New Mexico, you will be likely to find matters more lively."

"Can you help us in engaging the right parties?"

"I think so; call around at my office to-morrow afternoon, when I am quite sure I will be able to put you on the track of the ones whom you ought to meet."

The lads assured their host that they would be glad to do so, and, declining his kind invitation to spend the night at his home, bade him good-evening and started on their return to the Menger House.

CHAPTER III.

IN SAN ANTONIO.

NICK and Herbert stopped on the Plaza to inspect a bear, which a lank Texan had fastened to a staple by a rope, and was waiting thus late at night for a purchaser. The moment the boys passed, the owner began urging them to buy, offering the brute for fifteen dollars, and dwelling with much eloquence on the great bargain it was for anyone.

Our friends, however, had no use for any animals of that species, and, taking care to keep beyond reach of the beast, who showed a desire for closer acquaintance, they sauntered toward the hotel.

Just before reaching it, someone touched Nick's arm in such a timid manner that he turned, wondering what it could mean.

A lad about twelve years of age, ragged and the picture of distress, asked in a tremulous voice :

"Please, sir, you're from the North, aint you?"

"Yes," replied Nick; "is your home there?"

"Yes, sir," said the lad, swallowing a lump in his throat, "and I would give the world, if I had it, if I was back there again."

"How is it you're here?"

"Me and Dick Harrison run away from home; we lived in Philadelphia, and we haven't had anything to eat since yesterday."

"Where is Dick?"

"He's off yonder, on the other side of the Plaza; he's just dead broke up, and says he won't try nothin' more, but is goin' to lay down and die."

"I don't believe anyone has ever died of starvation in San Antonio; can't you get work?"

"We have been trying for two weeks; we got a job or two that fetched us a little to eat, but we can't do nothin' more."

"Take us over to where Dick is," said Herbert, whose heart was touched, "and let us see him."

"Come on," said the boy, so cheerfully that Nick and his friend were satisfied he was telling the truth. On the way across the Plaza, they questioned Fred Beekman, as he gave his name, still further.

"What made you run away from home, Fred?"

"Me and Dick started out to kill Injins and grizzly bears."

"How did you make out," asked Herbert, who recalled that it was not so long since he had indulged in similar ambitious ideas.

"We haven't killed any yet," replied Fred, in such a doleful voice that the others could not help smiling.

"How did you get the money to come to Texas?"

"Dick and me stole it from our folks; we bought rifles and pistols, but when we got to Texarkana we was took up and the guns took away from us; we managed to sneak off, and had enough money left to come to Santone; here it give out, and we've had it hard since."

"Had you pleasant homes?" asked Nick.

This question set Fred to crying. His

fingers were in his eyes, and he stumbled along for several paces before he could answer:

"Nobody ever had better homes, but we got it into our heads that it would be nice to shoot grizzly bears and Injins, and here we are. If we only had enough money to keep us from starvin' we could walk home like reg'lar tramps."

"You are a good many miles from Philadelphia," said Nick. "If you could get there, would you go straight home, or would you start off on some other wild-goose chase like this?"

"Oh, if I could see father and mother and my brother and two sisters, I would work and go to school and do anything; I never knowed how good a home I had till I run away, and Dick feels the same way."

A few minutes later they reached the spot where Dick had been left, but he was nowhere in sight. Fred looked around in wonder, and then became frightened.

"I'll bet he's gone and drownded hisself," he said, in an awed whisper, "for he felt 'nough like it."

"Boys like him don't drown themselves," replied Nick, who began to distrust the truthfulness of the lad; "if you want us to give you any help you must find Dick and bring him——"

"There he is!" broke in Fred, pointing to a figure lurking among the shadows some distance off, as if afraid to venture closer. "Here, Dick, come here! you needn't be scart, they won't hurt you!"

Seeing the lad approaching, Nick said: "Now, Fred, I don't want you to speak a word till I get through with Dick."

With considerable hesitation Dick ventured nearer, and Nick immediately took him in hand. After much questioning, he became convinced that the story told by the two was true. They were equally ragged and wretched looking, and, despite their coarse language, gave evidence of having belonged to good families.

Nick and Herbert provided them with an excellent supper. They were as ravenous as wild animals, and left no doubt that they were half famishing. Then, having made sure that they had a place to sleep during the night, Nick told them to call at the hotel in the morning, and he would see whether he and his friend could do anything for them.

During the interview, Nick managed to get the addresses of their parents in Philadelphia, without either suspecting his purpose. On reaching the Menger, he at once telegraphed to each father, asking whether a son whose name he gave was missing. He hardly doubted their story, but it was well that he took means to make sure, before acting upon that belief.

In the course of the evening, a reply came to each message, saying that the boys had been missing for six weeks, begging Nick to send both home without delay, and pledging that the expense would be paid by the senders of the telegrams, or, if desired, funds would be telegraphed. Nick notified the parents that the boys would start northward in the morning, and a statement of the money expended would be forwarded by mail.

When Fred and Dick presented themselves to Nick and Herbert, and were told that word had been received from their relatives, who would be delighted to receive them, they could hardly believe it, but were finally satisfied that there was no deception about it.

Herbert and Nick took the boys to a clothing establishment, where they were provided with comfortable outfits, a through ticket was furnished to each, enough money given to pay their expenses, and then, with a few words of counsel, they were despatched homeward, the happiest boys in the big State of Texas.

Then Nick inclosed the memoranda to the proper parties, and dismissed the subject from his mind, for weightier matters required attention.

Upon calling at the banker's office in the afternoon, they were surprised to find he had not only selected the two men that were to bear them company, but they were present, by appointment with Mr. Lord, who knew at what time the youths would arrive.

The individuals were typical cowboys, with their broad-brimmed sombreros and rattlesnake bands, their heavy shirts, trousers tucked in the tops of their boots, immense spurs, long wavy hair, handkerchiefs knotted about their necks, bright eyes and not unhandsome countenances.

Arden Strubell, the elder, was about thirty-five years of age and wore a long moustache and goatee, which, like his hair and eyes, were of a dark auburn. Baker Lattin, his companion, was a few years younger, with lighter hair, a faint moustache, no goatee, was wide across the temples, and his eyes were light blue or gray, but his appearance was as alert and intelligent as the other's.

These men were old friends of banker Lord, who had engaged with them upon several hunting excursions. It had fallen within his power to do for them a number of monetary favors, and they were the men who were ready to show their gratitude in any way he desired.

Strubell and Lattin intended to start in the course of a day or two for a ranch in New Mexico. They expected to travel the entire distance on horseback, accompanied by a single pack animal. Both once belonged to the mounted rangers of Texas, and had probably ridden over as much of that vast area as any other man within its limits, from No

Man's Land on the north, through the Pan Handle and across the Llano Estacado to the Rio Grande and the Pecos on the south and west.

Strubell had been in several brushes with the terrible Geronimo and his dusky desperadoes, but he did not expect to reach the section where there was danger of collision with them, their stamping ground being further to the west.

Banker Lord had been offered a ranch over the line in New Mexico, at such reasonable figures that he was much inclined to buy it, but, with his usual caution, he desired to know of a certainty its value before investing the money. Strubell and Lattin had been employed, therefore, to make a thorough examination and to report on the same to him.

This happened most opportunely for Nick and Herbert, who thus were furnished with the very best company on their long and dangerous ride through Western Texas, while the ranchmen were ordered to go with them, if necessary, beyond into Arizona and Southern California.

CHAPTER IV.

A STARTLING INTERRUPTION.

IT did not take the boys long to become acquainted with Strubell and Lattin. The former showed by his conversation that he possessed a fair education, though Lattin was barely able to write his name. They were frank, outspoken, courageous, ready of resource, familiar with all the dangers they were likely to meet on the long ride toward the northwest, and the finest horsemen the boys had ever seen.

Through the help of the Texans, Nick and Herbert secured three excellent animals, two of them possessing great speed and endurance, while the third was the equal of the best burro or mule for carrying a heavy burden. The Winchesters were the best, too, of their kind, the men being similarly armed. Nick and Herbert took care to provide themselves with an excellent field-glass apiece, for nothing was more likely than that they would find abundant call for their use. The rest of the supplies were bought on the advice of the cowboys.

They passed near a number of towns and settlements during the first week, in one of which they generally stayed overnight. So long as they were able to secure the comforts of ordinary travel through a settled section, they would have been foolish to decline it.

It had been so long since the boys had ridden far on horseback, that they were stiffened for the first few days, so that, when they dismounted, they were hardly able to walk. This, however, soon wore off until they were able to stand a ride of forty or fifty miles without any ill effects.

No physician could have watched a patient with greater care than Nick watched Herbert. He tried to keep it from the knowledge of his friend, and thought he succeeded, though Herbert told him afterward that he knew all the time what he was doing.

The elder youth felt bad when they reached St. Louis, and was still worse on their arrival

A STARTLING INTERRUPTION.

in San Antonio. The long ride in the cars made him feverish, and he had little appetite, but the new scenes and surroundings, the cheerful company of Nick, and his own ambition did wonders in the way of keeping him up.

He showed an improvement within twenty-four hours after arriving in the City of the Alamo, and this continued steadily, until the second day out, when the beautiful weather, that they had been having for weeks, was broken by a norther which, however, was not severe, though it brought so much rain and dismal weather that they were compelled to lie by at one of the straggling frontier towns for several days.

They rode through the hills and highlands between Fredericksburg and Fort Clark, fording a tributary of the Llano River, and pushing almost due northwest toward New Mexico, whose southeast corner they were aiming to strike at the point of intersection between the twenty-sixth meridian and thirty-second parallel.

The country now began to assume a wilder

appearance. The weather was like a dream, and Nick could well understand how it is that more than twenty thousand people in Texas never sleep under a roof from one year's end to another. He could appreciate, too, the reason why the immigrant, no matter how homesick, who braves it out for six months, never leaves Texas unless for a brief visit to his northern home, returning to die in the Lone Star State, which has become the land of his adoption.

The appearance showed the country, or rather that portion of it, to contain a great many more people than the boys supposed before entering Texas. The settlements were generally miserable collections of shanties, with the inevitable gambling and drinking saloon and the quota of "bad men," on the lookout for tenderfeet, or those of their own class that were ready to mingle in a row offhand. Everyone rode on horseback, and carried his revolver and rifle, the latter generally a Winchester of the repeating pattern.

The cattlemen were numerous, some of them nearly always in sight among the hills, or on the broad, rolling prairie. Occasionally an Indian was met, but he was far from being the romantic individual that boys generally have in mind, when reading about the noble red man. He was untidy and sullen looking, with an appetite for whiskey that was never sated, and the odor of rank tobacco around him.

It was about a week after the departure from San Antonio that the youths noticed a marked change in things. The country became more broken, the settlements disappeared, and during the middle of the afternoon, when Herbert swept the horizon with his field glass, he made known, with an expression of surprise, that there was not a living person, so far as he knew, in sight.

"We've put a good piece of country behind us," said Strubell, "and if nothing goes wrong, we ought to strike New Mexico in the course of the next ten days."

Nick laughed.

"I fancied we would make it in less time than that."

"So we mought," remarked Lattin, "if there was any call to hurry; but, as I understand this business, we aint runnin' the pony express for Santa Fé or Rincon."

That night their camp was in a section which charmed the boys, for there was an air of loneliness, and the danger that seemed to be brooding over the vicinity was of a kind not yet encountered since entering Texas.

In some respects, the camp reminded them of their moose hunt in Maine, though the contrast in the season was marked. There were the hills, rising almost to the dignity of mountains, the bowlders and rocks, the stream of water, not more than a few inches in width and depth, and the beautiful blue sky overhead.

The weather was cooler than it had been, and the hunters shook their heads, and hinted about a norther that was liable to break over them before many hours. There were no signs of Indians, and had there been, the aborigines would have been held in no greater dread than those of their own race. The party were so far westward that the arm of the law was weak, and everyone must depend on his own vigilance and alertness.

When the wood, which was not over abundant in those parts, was collected for the fire by which they intended to cook the meat obtained from a maverick earlier in the day, the horses were turned loose, and the four friends gathered around the blaze, which was kindled in an open space, where the light was visible for a long way in nearly every direction. Around this they sat, and, while the men smoked their pipes, they recalled many a thrilling encounter with the red men in the Pan Handle, in Arizona, and in New Mexico. Strubell and Lattin were equally interested in the story which Nick told of their hunt for the king of moose in Maine. That species of game was unfamiliar to them, and when they learned of the gallant style in which Herbert brought down the big fellow at the moment he was charging upon his companion, they looked upon the tall youth with something like wonder and admiration. They had no idea of having such a hero "in their midst."

Since it was necessary that everyone should bear a hand in guarding against the perils on which they were entering, the hunters arranged that the youths should regularly take part in standing watch each night. Their method made it easy and safe for all, since the watches were four in number, each about two hours long. Everyone was able to keep awake for that length of time, even while sitting on the ground, and the turns alternated, so as to equalize the task all round. Had the watches been longer, the youths, as was the case while down East, would have been likely to slumber on their posts.

Arden Strubell was stretched out on the further side of the fire, flat on his back, his head resting on a stone, which was softened somewhat by his hands that were clasped between it and the back of his head, with the elbows projecting like wings from each side. One leg was partly drawn up, with the other crossed over it, his position being the picture of indolence and ease. The pipe, whose stem was in the corner of his mouth, was only gently puffed at long intervals, for it was Arden's turn to sleep until eleven o'clock. He was, therefore, taking no share in the conversation which went on in such gentle, murmuring tones that it tended more to drowsiness than wakefulness on his part.

Matters were in this form, and the night was progressing, when Lattin, who was sitting directly opposite his friend, raised his hand for silence, and said in a frightened whisper:

"Arden, don't move or you're a dead man!"

"I know it," was the quiet reply from the Texan, who did not stir a muscle, "but what can I do? I'm a dead man anyway."

CHAPTER V.

A TEST OF ONE'S NERVES.

NICK RIBSAM and Herbert Watrous could hardly believe their own senses, and for a second or two looked at each other and at the cowboys, to make sure they had heard aright.

The youths were lolling near each other, Nick leaning on his elbow and looking in the broad face of Lattin, who just then was telling of a scrimmage in which he had had the closest call of his life while hunting Geronimo, while Herbert sat more erect.

Strubell, as has been told, was lying on his back on the other side of the camp fire, his hands clasped behind his head, and resting on his stone pillow. His sombrero lay on his forehead, in such a way that a part of the rim shaded his eyes, whose view of the outer world was obtained by gazing down along the front of his face and chin. He could see his slowly

A TEST OF ONE'S NERVES.

heaving breast, the cartridge belt, and the one leg crossed over the other and partly crooked at the knee. Off to the left was the glowing camp fire, and, by turning his eyes without moving his head, he could trace a part of the figure of Lattin, who was discoursing for the entertainment of his young friends.

This was the shape of matters, when the younger cowboy abruptly checked his narrative, and, looking across the fire at his companion, warned him not to move on the penalty of instant death, to which the other, without stirring a muscle or giving any evidence of alarm, calmly replied that he was aware of his situation, which was so hopeless that he considered himself the same as dead already.

"Don't move," added Lattin in a whisper to the boys, "or you will scare it; keep on talking the same as before, and maybe it will let him alone."

"What are you referring to?" asked the perplexed Nick.

"There's a tarantula lying on Arden's breast; don't you see it?"

The hideous thing was sitting on the chest

of the cowboy, directly over his heart. Where it had come from no one could say, but probably the warmth of the fire or that of the body of the Texan had drawn it to the spot, and it was now making an exploration, on its own account, ready to inflict its deadly bite on the least provocation.

Strubell was half asleep, when, looking along the front of his body, he saw the outlines of the spider in the yellow light of the camp fire. It caused a slight tickling sensation, as it slowly felt its way forward. He knew its nature the instant he caught sight of it, and he observed that it was of unusual size and fierceness. He had seen a comrade die from the bite of a tarantula, which is held in greater dread than the famous rattlers of Texas, for it gives no warning of its intentions, which most frequently come in the form of a nipping bite whose effects are not only fatal but frightfully rapid.

Arden might have slowly unclasped his hands and given the thing a quick flirt, but the chances were a thousand to one that, if he did so, it would bite his finger. If let alone, it might change its purpose and crawl off into the darkness. It was not likely to injure him so long as it stayed on the front of his shirt, for it was hard for it to bite through that. It preferred the naked surface of the body in order to do its worst.

It could not very well bite the hands, since they remained clasped behind the Texan's head. The nearest favorable points were the neck, where the shirt was open, and the face. If the spider crept upward, it was evident that it was making for one or the other, and there seemed no way of checking it, for the first move on the part of any one of the friends would rouse its anger, and cause it to bite the man on whose body it was resting. All that could be done was to do nothing, and pray to Heaven to save the poor fellow from impending death.

"We mustn't show by anything we do," said Lattin, "that we are excited. A quick move—a loud call, or any unusual motion may lead it to use its teeth. It's the biggest and ugliest tarantula that I ever laid eyes on, and if it gives Arden one nip, he's a goner."

"But it is terrible to sit here and see him die," said Nick, who was so nervous he found it hard to remain still, while Herbert trembled as if with a chill.

"It's all we can do," replied the Texan, who nevertheless kept a sharp eye on the thing, as if he was meditating some desperate resort to save his comrade's life. "We will talk on, as though nothing has took place out of the usual run, and while we're at it we'll keep an eye on the critter."

"What good will it do to keep an eye on it," was the sensible question of Nick, "if we do nothing?"

"Leave that to me and don't either of you stir. You know that we're on our way to look after a ranch that Mr. Lord thinks of buying in New Mexico?"

He paused and gazed at the boys, as if in doubt whether they understood the matter. They nodded their heads and he continued:

"George Jennings owns the ranch and wants to move east. Last year he had another in Arizona. It was too small to suit him, and he came over this way, and now, as I said, wants to get out of the bus'ness altogether. You know, I s'pose, that they have warm weather in Arizona at certain times in the year?"

Once more the cowboy checked himself, as if he desired a reply. He seemed to be looking at the boys, but in reality was watching the tarantula, which was motionless on the breast of Strubell, as if he, too, was debating what was best to do.

"I don't know of any part of the country where they do not have pretty hot weather in the course of the year," said Nick.

"But Arizona lays over 'em all," said Lattin, as if proud of the fact; "I've seen it day after day there, and night, too, when the thermometer doesn't get below a hundred. Wal, it was on one of them blazing afternoons, that Jennings stretched out on the floor in his low front room to take a nap. His wife had gone to San Pedro a couple of days before, under the escort of the two ranchmen hired by him, and he was looking for 'em back every hour.

"That's the way it came about that the

father was left with his little gal Mabel, which was only six years old. Jennings loved that gal more than the apple of his eye, and would give his life any time to keep her from harm. I b'lieve you've a little sister, Nick, that you think a good deal of?"

"I have, God bless her!" replied Nick, as the moisture crept in his eyes; "there is nothing I would not do to save her from suffering and pain."

Again, Lattin seemed to be looking at the countenance of the honest youth, but in reality his eyes were on the tarantula, and his right hand was moving slowly down his side toward his revolver in the belt at his waist.

"That bein' so, you can understand how much Jennings thought of his little gal Mabel. Wal, he was in the middle of a nap, when he jumped to his feet as if he had seen a rattler crawling over the floor toward him. The reason why he jumped up so quick was 'cause he heard his little gal scream. He went out the door as if shot from the mouth of a cannon.

"The sight that met the ranchman was

enough to set any father wild. Two of Geronimo's Apaches, each on a pony, was galloping off on a dead run. One of them held Mabel in his arms, and the little gal, at sight of her father, reached out her arms and called to him to come and take her away from the bad Injun. Don't you think that was enough to turn a father's brain?"

"There can be no doubt of that," replied Nick, shuddering at the mental picture of his sister Nellie in such an awful situation.

During the momentary pause, Lattin placed his hand on the butt of his revolver. The tarantula had not stirred more than an inch since he was seen, but that was in the direction of the Texan's face, and his peril was becoming more imminent than before.

"Be careful, boys," said Strubell in his ordinary tones, "the creature is getting nervous. He is now looking at me, and is coming a little closer to my face. Don't try to brush or knock him off: maybe he'll hunt for some other pasture, but the chances are against it."

"All right, Ard," replied Lattin with assumed cheerfulness; "we see your fix and are prayin' for you. As I was sayin', the sight that met Jennings' eyes, when he jumped out of his door, was enough to set any man frantic. He was back into the house again, and out once more like a flash. He had his Winchester with him this time, and brought it to his shoulder, but the Apache that had his little gal was on the watch and held her up in front, so that the father couldn't fire without killing his own child. So Jennings just give one groan and staggered back into the house and almost fell on to the floor.

"The poor fellow was in a bad fix. The nearest fort was a hundred miles off, and it was almost as far to San Pedro. The two Apaches had rode to the ranch on one pony, but, when they went away, the one that didn't have the little gal was on the back of Jennings' horse, and, since his wife and escort was absent, there wasn't a single critter on the place.

"The first Apache had got so far off that he was beyond rifle-shot before Jennings was outdoors. He come out a few minutes later, and, shading his eyes, looked off across the dusty plain, where his child had disappeared. He thought the horses which he seen were growing plainer. They were coming toward him, and he didn't know what it meant.

"For a while he didn't stir, but kept looking closely. Bimeby, he seen there was but one horseman and he was Sam Ruggles, one of them that had acted as the escort of Mrs. Jennings when she went away. He was mounted on his own horse, and leading that of Mrs. Jennings, who he said would start home the next day.

"'The country is so open,' said Sam, 'that she thought I had better start at once, so as to give you what help I could with the cattle—what's the matter, George?' he asked, observing the white face of his friend.

"'Where did you get my horse?' asked Jennings, striving hard to control himself.

"'Up near the ford,' said Sam; 'just as I stopped to let my pony drink, someone fired at me from the bush, and I dropped out the saddle to the ground. I wasn't hurt a bit; it was a dodge of mine to trick the redskin. The next instant, there was a whoop, and an Apache galloped out of the bush toward me, sure of another scalp. Wal,' added Sam, with a grin, 'an Apache can mistake, the same as other folks, and I needn't give you the partic'lars. Your horse seemed to think he was at liberty to travel home, and he went so fast that I didn't overhaul him till about a mile out. I was worried thinkin' something had happened, and was glad enough to see that everything was right.' Now that was a big mistake of Sam, wasn't it?"

Nick and Herbert turned toward the speaker, as both answered his odd question, and observed that he now held his revolver in hand.

"Boys," called poor Strubell, "the tarantula is creeping toward my face; I guess he means to bite; don't stir, and if he gets much closer I'll make a sweep at him."

CHAPTER VI.

TWO GOOD SHOTS.

"WAL, then, Jennings tells Sam everything that had took place. It was wonderful the control the ranchman showed over himself. His face was as white as death, but he didn't tremble, and talked as if he was speaking about the cattle. Sam thought that the Apache, having the extra load of the child and dead warrior, would not be able to travel fast, and there was a chance of fetching him off his pony, but Jennings feared there was a party of the varmints near by, and that he would jine them.

"Howsumever, you may be sure they didn't lose any time talking, but jumping into their saddles, was off across the plain like a couple of whirlwinds. The trail showed that the Apache, with the gal and dead warrior, had kept close to the bushes that grew along the stream, which was not very broad, and runs into the Gila.

"A mile from the ford the two were surprised to come upon the body of the Apache that had been tumbled from the horse by Sam's Winchester. The other must have got tired of carrying him, or was afraid his load would get him into trouble.

"'At any rate,' said the father, 'Mabel is alive, though there's no sayin' how long she will stay so.'

"Just then both catched sight of the very Apache they was after. He was coming from the bush on a swift gallop, and still holding the crying child in front of him.

"Now, that Apache showed less cunning than is generally showed by his people, for, by thus hanging back, he gave the pursuers the very chance they wanted to come up with him. Even then he had so little fear that Jennings and Sam believed there was a party near at hand, though, as it turned out, it wasn't so.

"As he come out of the bush, he struck across the open plain, with his pony on a sharp gallop, while little Mabel, seeing her father, stretched out her arms agin toward him and begged him to take her home.

"'Leave him to me,' said Jennings, bringing his Winchester to his shoulder. The redskin raised the child again, but he was just a second too late, for he rolled off his horse with a hole bored through his skull, as dead as dead could be.

"Mabel was bruised by her fall, but the Apache was killed so quick that he hadn't a chance to put her out of the way, as he would have done had he knowed what was comin'. She was soon in her father's arms, and all come out right as it does in the stories."

Despite the interest in the incidents related by the Texan, the eyes of all three were fixed on the dreaded tarantula, which had been comparatively motionless for some minutes. It now began creeping toward the face of Strubell, who said in the same unwavering voice:

"He's coming this time sure! He means to bite, boys, and it's all up with me——"

At that instant, the oppressive stillness was broken by the sharp report of Lattin's revolver, which he had extracted from his belt a few seconds before. He levelled and fired the weapon with such marvellous quickness that his friends hardly caught the movement.

But the aim was perfect. The tarantula that was straddling across the chest of the prostrate Texan, surcharged with virus and about to inflict its fatal bite, vanished as though it had never been. There was a faint whiz, and it was gone into nothingness.

Arden Strubell did not stir, but remained with his hands clasped behind his head and every muscle motionless. Then, as his comrade pronounced his name, his elbows fell and the head partly rolled to one side.

"By George!" exclaimed Lattin, springing up, "that's the first time I ever seen Ard faint away."

"I don't wonder that he did!" said Nick, as he and Herbert also hurried to his relief.

They were hardly at his side and stooping over him, when he opened his eyes with a wan smile, and said faintly:

"It seems to have been a little too much for me, boys."

But he quickly rallied and assumed the sitting position.

"I had just made up my mind to give the spider a flirt with my hat," he said, "but the tarantula is so quick, I knew it would get in its work before I could brush it off. If I had struck at it with my hat when I first saw it there would have been an even chance, but I felt as though my arms were made of iron, and I was like a man with the nightmare, who cannot force his limbs to move. That was a good shot of yours, Baker."

"I'm rather proud of it," replied Lattin, settling back on his blanket, "and I thought it must come to that from the first, but I was so afraid of missing, that I put it off to the last second. If I had failed, the report would have started it into bitin' you before I could give it a second shot."

"I wonder whether there are any more of them around," said Herbert, glancing furtively about.

"That's what has troubled me," added Nick.

"I don't think any more of them will

bother us," remarked Strubell, quick to recover from his fright; "we must expect these little annoyances in this part of the world."

"Yes," observed Lattin, "when you find such a fine climate as we have, and everything else just right to make you the happiest chap in the United States, which means the happiest in the world, you oughter be willing to pay for it."

"Well," said Nick, who, now that the oppressive burden was lifted, could smile at the conceits of his friends, "when we come to add the sum total, it will be found pretty much the same the world over. It seems to me, after the fright we have all had, that none of us will be able to sleep."

"What time is it?" asked Strubell. Nick looked at his watch, and replied that it was near eleven o'clock.

The Texan gathered the folds of his blanket around him, turned on his side, and within five minutes was asleep. The youths were amazed, but, as Lattin remarked, it was all easy enough when you became used to it.

It was the place of Herbert to watch over the camp from eleven until one o'clock, at which hour Nick would take his turn, Lattin and Strubell following in turn. The former willingly kept company with the boys while they discussed the startling occurrence early in the evening. By and by, however, the Texan became drowsy, and, bidding his young friends good-night, he too gathered his thick blanket about his muscular form, and joined his comrade in the land of dreams.

When Herbert took out his handsome watch to wind it, he leaned forward, so that the light from the fire fell upon its face. It happened that both hands were exactly together at the figure twelve, so that it was midnight and his duty was half over.

He looked round at the impressive scene. The fire was burning cheerily, though with the help of their thick, serviceable blankets the warmth was not needed. The horses were lying down, or cropping the grass, which was not very abundant in the immediate vicinity, and were too far off in the gloom to be seen. Each of his friends was so swathed that he resembled a log of wood when viewed from a short distance. The feet of all were turned toward the blaze, that being the general rule when sleeping in camp. The saddles, rifles, and extra luggage were loosely piled at one side, and Herbert, who was always inclined to be pressed down by his responsibility at such a time, could not help reflecting how completely a party of Indians or outlaws could place the hunters at their mercy by a sudden dash from the gloom.

But that kind of danger was not thought of by either of the Texans, who were not riding though this section for the first time.

It was only a few minutes later that Herbert heard one of the horses emit a slight whinny, as if something had disturbed him. The youth peered in the direction whence it came, but there was no moon and he discerned nothing.

"I wonder what it is," he said, pressing his Winchester to make sure it was actually within his grasp; "it may be another tarantula, a rattlesnake, a bear, or some other wild animal or wild person trying to steal into camp without alarming us."

One of the other ponies snuffed the air, the noise being as distinct in the stillness as was the sound of his watch when he wound it.

Herbert would not have been blamed had he awakened Strubell or Lattin, but he decided to wait before doing so. There was barely a possibility of peril from Indians or white men, and he considered himself able to meet any other kind.

The air, that had been oppressively still, was stirred by a breath which brought to him a peculiar sound. It lasted only a moment, and resembled the faint tapping of myriads of hammers on the earth—so numerous indeed that he suspected its meaning.

Applying his ear to the ground, he caught it with greater distinctness. It was as he supposed: an immense number of cattle were galloping over the plain, beyond the hills. They might be on their way to water or had been startled by some trivial cause, which often stampedes a drove that numbers thousands.

"Now if I find they are coming this way,"

thought the youth, "I will wake Strubell. They wouldn't be likely to enter the hills and run over this fire, but they might make trouble for our ponies."

At intervals of a few minutes he pressed his ear to the earth as before, and listened closely. The second time he did so he was certain the peculiar sounds were more distinct; but, waiting a brief while, he tried it again, and concluded they were neither louder nor fainter.

"They can't be standing still," was his logical conclusion, "and must soon come nearer or go further off."

Only a few minutes were required to settle the question: the cattle were receding, and doing so with such rapidity, that, much sooner than would have been suspected, the sounds had died out altogether.

CHAPTER VII.

AN INTRUDER IN CAMP.

THE minutes pass slowly at such times, and, though Herbert's duty lasted only two hours, they seemed double the length of that period during the day, or when his companions were awake.

The listening ear caught no further sounds of the multitudinous feet, and he dismissed the matter from his mind. The still air now and then was moved by what seemed a slight breeze, or eddy of wind, but it was barely sufficient to stir the blaze. Once he heard the report of a gun, startlingly distinct, though he knew it might have been fired fully a mile away.

"We are not the only people in this part of the world," he mused, giving expression to his reveries; "and that shot may have ended the life of some person."

It was a disturbing thought, and, as if to

drive off the oppressiveness that was weighing him down, he rose to his feet and threw more sticks on the flames. His watch showed that it was only half-past twelve. He held the time-piece to his ear, suspecting that it had stopped running; but the familiar ticking was audible, and a glance at the tiny second-hand showed that it was really moving, though it never seemed to creep so tardily around the little circle.

Then he watched the indicator as it marked its course, and resorted to the many artifices that occur to those who find time dragging wearily on their hands. No hour ever seemed longer than was required for the watch to show that a fourth of that time had passed forever.

"But it will be worse for Nick," he concluded; "I think his task more wearisome than mine. We have all to take our share, however, as I suppose everyone must in the good and bad of life."

Herbert waited till the full time was up, and several minutes over, when he stepped to where Nick was lying, and gently shook his shoulder. He awoke readily, prepared to act his part as sentinel for the next two hours.

The elder told his friend what had occurred, adding that he discovered nothing else to disturb him. Then bidding him good-night, he wrapped himself in his own blanket and lay down with his feet toward the fire, falling asleep almost as quickly as had the cowboys before him.

Nick examined his rifle and saw it was ready for instant service, as was his pistol, with which he had practised until quite expert in its use. He sat down just beyond the circle of illumination thrown out by the blaze, for, somehow or other, it always seemed to him that such a course was not only safer, but that he could maintain more effective watch by doing so. He was able to see every one of his friends, while a prowler was not likely to observe him, unless his approach to camp was such as to place the guardsman between him and the blaze. In that event, he was quite sure to notice his outlines against the fire.

That this was a wise proceeding was proven by what followed.

He had been on duty for a half hour or more when he was disturbed by the same cause that startled Herbert. One of the horses uttered a slight neigh, giving no other evidence of alarm, if that was the meaning of the sound.

At this moment Nick was well back, on the opposite of the camp from the animals. He was therefore confident that if anything threatened them, he himself was invisible to whatever it might be.

After listening a few minutes, he decided to investigate for himself. This he did, not by proceeding in a direct line, as he could have done, but by making a circle which took him beyond the light of the fire until nigh enough to observe the animals.

They were on the ground, as though they had cropped their fill, and now enjoyed rest more than food. They appeared to be reposing quietly, and he concluded that the slight noise which he had noticed signified nothing. Horses and other domestic animals often start in their sleep, as though disturbed by dreams, the same as do we, and that which

AN INTRUDER IN CAMP. 63

Nick heard may have been evidence of the fact.

Still, it is also a truth that men, when in situations of peril, frequently find it safer to rely more on the acuteness of their horse than upon their own vigilance. The animal seems to have his senses sharpened to the finest point, for his master's good.

"I guess there's nothing wrong," said Nick to himself, after inspecting the ponies; "but it is best to act as though danger always threatens. That's what Strubell and Lattin say, and everyone must see its logic."

The fire was now burning so low that he gathered up a lot of wood and threw it on the flames. While thus employed, his gun lay on the ground near the feet of Herbert. The thought that, if any hostile prowler was near, it was the easiest thing in the world to pick him off, caused a strange feeling to come over the youthful sentinel, and his relief was great when able to catch up his gun and slip back in the protecting gloom of the night.

He had taken occasion, while near the fire, to glance at his watch, and, like his companion, was astonished to learn how brief the time was that he had been on duty. It was less than half an hour.

About the same period passed without the most trifling alarm. Nick studiously held himself in the background, where he moved slowly about, dreading to sit down, though often tempted to do so. He knew that so long as he kept the erect posture his senses would be at command, and it was far easier to do this by motion, no matter how slight, than by standing still.

He had reached the conclusion that the night was to be as uneventful as those that had preceded it, when once more one of the ponies uttered the same sound that had disturbed him before. Nick was startled, for the belief flashed upon him that this signified something. There must be some cause for the alarm of the animals, outside of themselves.

He reflected for a minute upon the most prudent thing to do. He dismissed the thought of awaking the Texans, for, like Herbert, he shrank from asking their help until certain it was needed, for, by so doing, he confessed his own inability to meet the danger, whatever it might be.

He now determined to make a much larger circuit than before, his object being to bring the horses between him and the fire. This would not only show the animals, but was likely to reveal the disturbing cause. At the same time, Nick himself could remain in the gloom, where it was hardly possible to be seen. The moon, which might have interfered with the success of this plan, would not be above the horizon for several hours to come.

In order to traverse the distance he had in mind, he was forced to move around several large rocks and bowlders, cross the small stream which flowed near the camp, and pick his way with the utmost care. Stillness was necessary above all things.

The darkness, while favorable in many respects, had its disadvantages, as was quickly proven. At the moment when he believed he was opposite the ponies, and, therefore, near them, he stepped upon a rolling stone, and despite his expertness, fell with a thump to the ground.

He was impatient with himself, and could hardly repress an angry exclamation, for a snuff from one of the animals showed how alert they were to the slightest disturbance.

"The next thing to be done," reflected Nick, "is to shoot off my rifle; then the job will be in fine shape."

But, so far as he could judge, no harm had been done, and he pressed on with greater care than before. It took considerable time to reach the desired point, but it was attained at last. The horses were in a direct line with the camp fire, and he began stealing toward them.

This was the time for extreme caution, for, if the least noise betrayed him, all chance of success would be destroyed. It may be doubted, however, whether either of the Texans himself could have carried out the plan more skilfully than did Nick Ribsam.

When he halted, he was not fifty feet from his own animal, and had approached him so silently that no one of the ponies was disturbed. They were silent, as if asleep.

But at the moment when Nick was motionless and carefully studying the dark figures, whose upper parts were shown against the background of the fire, he saw one of the animals raise his head higher than the others and emit a snuff, louder than ever.

"It couldn't be that I caused that," was the decision of Nick, who was in a crouching posture; "it's something else that alarmed them, and, whatever it is, it is closer to them than I am."

He was right, for hardly had he begun creeping forward, when the head and shoulders of a man slowly rose between him and the horses, and in a direct line with the camp fire, which revealed the upper part of his body as distinctly as if stamped with ink against the yellow background of flame.

"It's a white man," was Nick's conclusion. "and he is there for no good."

The presence of the intruder now helped the youth in his hurried but stealthy approach; for, when the horses showed additional excitement, perhaps, at the coming of a second person, the stranger would believe it was caused wholly by himself. Apprehending no approach, too, from the rear, he would give no attention to that direction, but keep his eye on the camp to be ready for any demonstration from that quarter.

It is quite possible that he saw Nick when he withdrew beyond the light, but he had no reason to suspect he had flanked him and passed round to the other side.

It took the sentinel but a few more minutes to satisfy himself of the errand of the intruder. Nick's own pony was approached and obliged to rise to his feet. The stranger was a horse thief, making a stealthy raid upon the camp, while all the campers but one were asleep.

Taking the head of Nick's horse, he was in the act of flinging himself upon his bare back, when the youth stepped forward in the gloom and called out:

"*Hands up, quicker than lightning!*"

Nick imitated as nearly as he could the voice and manner of one of the Texans when making a similar startling demand.

CHAPTER VIII.

BELL RICKARD.

NICK RIBSAM had no wish to figure as a rough border character, who ordered his captive to "throw up his hands," when able to secure "the drop on him"; but the youth had the native shrewdness to suit himself to the situation. He and Herbert had been in the Lone Star State long enough to pick up a good deal of information.

When he discovered the stranger among the horses, there could be hardly a doubt of his business, but he waited till he was in the act of riding off with his own horse before he called out the startling words which told the thief he was caught.

A man who is used to getting the drop on others is quite sure to know when that little point is made on him. The intruder was on the point of leaping upon the back of Nick's pony, but checked himself and promptly reached both hands upward.

"You've got the drop on me, pard, this time, but go easy," said he in a voice as cheery as if he were talking about the weather.

"Face toward the fire, walk straight forward and don't stop, turn round, or try anything till you get the word from me."

All this time, the thief was striving to gain a sight of the individual who held him at his mercy. It was evident he did not recognize the voice, and there may have been something in Nick's tones which led him to think he was not a full grown man. He was standing erect, with his Winchester levelled, and nothing in the world was easier than for him to send a bullet through his body.

Border law never would have questioned the act: rather it would have blamed him for showing mercy. But Nick Ribsam, like every right-thinking person, looked upon the taking of human life in its true light, and as never right unless to save his own. The man before him was trying to steal his property, but nothing more. No doubt he would have been quick to shoot Nick if their situations were reversed, but this could not affect the views of the youth. As yet he had no right to harm him.

Nick assumed a ferocity that he was far from feeling. He was playing a part, and doing it well.

When the thief heard the command, he hesitated, as if unwilling to obey it.

"I guess you hadn't better insist on *that*," he said, with a half laugh, full of significance.

"What do you mean, sir?"

"If you start to foller me to the camp, my pard, just behind you, will give it to you in the neck."

This was alarming, and for a moment Nick was in doubt what to do. If he should start to drive the horse thief before him, only to find that his armed companion was doing the same with him, the tables would be turned in the highest style of the art.

But the youth's brightness came to his aid. He knew that if this man had a comrade in his wrong doing, he would have put in an appearance before matters had reached this interesting stage: he never would have remained in the background, while Nick was securing the drop on the other.

He had no one with him. He was alone, and was trying a trick on his captor.

"Walk on," said Nick; "when your partner shows up, we'll attend to *his* case."

The rogue saw there was no help for it, and, without another word of protest, walked sullenly in the direction of the camp fire.

The prisoner seemed to have concluded that, inasmuch as he had to submit, his true plan was to do so gracefully. He walked with a certain dignity along the line pointed out, while Nick kept a few paces to the rear, with his Winchester ready for instant call.

It was the first time he was ever placed in such a situation, and, as may be supposed, his emotions were peculiar. As the figure in front grew more distinct in the light of the camp fire, he saw that he was of unusual size, being at at least six feet tall, long-limbed, and thin of frame. There could be no doubt he was fully armed, with the exception of a rifle, which, for some reason or other, was absent. He had probably left it near by, in order that nothing might hinder the best use of his arms while committing his crime.

Nick cleverly shortened the space separating them, for he was afraid of some trick on the part of his captive. The scamp might open on the sleeping cowboys and riddle them before he could prevent. But such fears were causeless. A course of that kind, as he himself well knew, would insure his instant death at the hands of his captor. It would have been more reasonable had he turned like a flash, when in the partial gloom, and let fly at Nick, instead of pointing both hands at the stars with such readiness when ordered so to do.

Had the fellow known what he learned a few minutes later, he would have done that very thing, and with almost certain success; for his revolver could have been drawn and fired before the youth would have suspected what was going on.

At the moment the stranger came into full view, near the fire and the sleepers, his captor called:

"Halt! that will do!"

To Nick's astonishment he saw two figures rise like shadows from the ground. They were Strubell and Lattin, who, flinging off their blankets, stood each with revolver in hand, ready for business. In fact, the loud call of Nick was meant to awaken one or both of them, for matters were assuming that shape that the young man felt he must have their help at once.

His loud summons, however, was unnecessary, for the words which had already passed between the captor and his prisoner had brought them to their senses. Men like them are light sleepers, and they were quick to discover what was going on. More than that, they recognized the voice of the intruder as that of Bell Rickard, one of the most desperate horse thieves in the Southwest.

Had the fellow tried the trick on Nick, the Texans held themselves prepared to bound into the affray, and rush it to a conclusion like a cyclone, but the words they overheard gave them a clue to what was going on. They saw that the great connoisseur in horse flesh had put his foot in it in the worst kind of a way. He was in the power of a boy, who had actually made him a prisoner—a feat which the sheriffs of half a dozen counties had been trying for months in vain to do.

They hardly expected Nick to bring him into camp without trouble; and though Strubell and Lattin lay motionless on the ground, listening and awaiting events, they had loosened their blankets, drawn their weapons, and were on the alert.

But the great Rickard, at the moment of halting, found himself face to face with the two cowboys, whom he had known well for several years, and with whom he had exchanged more than one shot, each fired with the intent to kill.

"Howdy, Bell?" said Strubell, with a smile on his handsome face which had a world of meaning; "I hope you feel well, pard."

"Tollyble, thank you," replied the rogue, extending his hand to each of the cowboys in turn; "how is it with you?"

Lattin answered for both that they were well, and then invited the new arrival to a seat by the fire. Rickard returned thanks as courteously as if he were receiving the greatest favor that could be granted him.

The next moment the three were lolling side by side, as smiling and seemingly on as good terms as though they were brothers. Bell carried his brierwood with him, and Strubell passed him his little sack of tobacco, from which he helped himself, the party mingling their smoke, smiling and even laughing at the jocose remarks that were passed.

Herbert Watrous slept on, undisturbed by the noise, while Nick Ribsam stood in the background, viewing the scene, which impressed him as the most extraordinary he had ever witnessed.

"Let me see," said Lattin reflectively, "it's several months since we last met: do you remember where it was?"

"I think," replied Rickard, looking thoughtfully at the stars, as if busy with memory, "that it was in Laredo, at Brown's place."

"You're right," struck in the cowboy; "we had a shooting scrap, and I came near passing in my checks."

"Yes," laughed Bell, "I thought I had you that time, but I fired too quick; the lights went out, and then the room was full of smoke and bullets. When things cleared up, you wasn't there."

"No," said Lattin, "you folks were too thick for me, and I lit out; I swum the Rio Grande, just as Ben Thompson did when he got catched in the same place and in the same way. He got off without a scratch, as he did hundreds of times before, only to catch it at Santone at last, as he was bound to do sooner or later."

CHAPTER IX.

DEPARTURE OF THE GUEST.

"BEN and me done travelled a good deal together," said Rickard, with a faint sigh; "he was the quickest chap on the shoot I ever met; I never knowed him to miss when he had any show at all, and he was the luckiest fellow that ever walked. Do you know what Ben's rule was?" asked Rickard, turning toward the cowboys, as if about to impart a piece of delightful news.

"It was to shoot whenever he had the slightest excuse," replied Strubell, who evidently had little respect for one of the most famous characters that Texas ever brought to the surface.

"Whenever he got into a shooting scrap he always let the other chap fire first; for then, when *he* let fly, he had a good case of self-defence. He always done that, as he told me himself."

I may be allowed to say that this remark about Ben Thompson, once City Marshal of Austin, was true. He informed me that he had followed the rule for years, and it doubtless helped to secure his acquittal in a large number of the cases where he was tried for slaying others, though the shameful admiration shown him by all classes had much to do with his immunity from legal punishment. As has been hinted, however, there came a time when Ben's rule failed to work satisfactorily for himself. It was down in San Antonio, the scene of more than one of his crimes, that a half dozen men worked in a volley from their Winchesters ahead of Ben's revolver, and he died with his boots on, the last shot which he fired before breathing his last causing the death of one of his assailants.

It is hardly worth while to give the conversation which went on by the camp fire for fully two hours, for it was not of a character that can be commended to readers. There were stirring reminiscences of those "bad men," known a few years ago respectively as Bill Longley and John Wesley Hardin. I suppose that Texas never produced two more desperate men. When I saw Longley, he was as handsome a person as I ever met, and proved to be one of the few legally hanged individuals in the Lone Star State, his taking off occurring some years ago in Galveston.

Hardin was more ill-favored, as to personal appearance. He was the son of a preacher, and was named for one of the great founders of Methodism. When I last talked with the stumpy, broad-faced desperado he was in the Austin penitentiary, serving a twenty-five years' sentence for horse stealing, the numerous capital crimes he had committed not being taken into account.

The point I am making is that Bell Rickard, who, in his way, was as evil a man as any one of those whom I have named, having entered the camp as a prisoner, was treated as a guest. No one unacquainted with the circumstances would have suspected there was any feeling other than the strongest friendship between them.

They recalled the numerous stirring scrimmages in which they had taken part, and generally with Strubell and Lattin as the deadly enemies of Rickard and his friends. They laughed over the many close calls, when their mutual escapes seemed to turn on a hair, and even referred to those that were likely to occur again in the near future.

Nick Ribsam grew so interested that he forgot his duty as sentinel, and, leaning on his gun, stared with open mouth at the attenuated Texan, with his scraggly beard, restless gray eyes, and alert movements, as he smoked and laughed and talked.

Suddenly Strubell turned to the youth and said:

"Nick, I guess you had better take a look at the animals; Bell may have some friends around; if you get sight of any, don't bother to ask questions, but drop them at the first shot."

Rickard stopped in the middle of a remark he was making, and looked at the young man with a smile. Then he resumed his words, and the conversation went on as before. Nick walked slowly out to where the ponies were lying on the ground, wondering and puzzled by the new phase of southwestern life as he saw it for the first time.

"Wal," said Rickard, after talking a while longer, as he rose to his feet, stretched his limbs, and yawned, "I guess I'll have to be going, pards. By-by."

"By-by," returned Strubell and Lattin, the latter adding:

"Take good care of yourself, Bell, till we meet again."

"The same to you," he returned, moving off in the darkness at a leisurely gait, which showed that personal danger was the last thought that entered his mind.

Nick Ribsam, who was still standing near the animals, saw the tall figure, with slightly stooping shoulders, approaching.

"Helloa, younker, where are you?" he asked, coming to a halt and peering round in the gloom, his opportunity for seeing the youth being less favorable than that of Nick for observing him.

"I am here," replied the lad, holding his Winchester in a tight grip and apprehensive of trouble.

DEPARTURE OF THE GUEST.

"I only wanted to say good-by to you; I think you and me will meet before many days; till then, the best of luck to you."

"The same to yourself," replied Nick, who kept his eyes on the fellow until he mingled with the gloom and became invisible.

Then he walked back to the camp fire, in answer to a whistle from Strubell, who asked the time. It was not quite three o'clock, but was so near that hour that the elder Texan told him to lie down while he and Lattin looked after things for the rest of the night.

Nick hoped his friends would give an explanation of the strange occurrence, but, though he waited several minutes, no reference was made to it, and he lay down in his blanket beside the sleeping Herbert, who had not once opened his eyes.

It was some time before the youth became unconscious, for he was affected by what he had seen and heard. He was convinced that, however friendly the feeling appeared to be between the Texans and their visitor, the latter was a deadly enemy of himself. He believed, too, that Rickard's parting words contained a threat, and he was sure there would be a meeting between them before many days.

Finally slumber overcame him and he did not awake until he heard the voice of Herbert, and all were astir, with day fully come.

Strubell was busy preparing coffee over the coals, and cooking the remains of the maverick shot the day before. The climate and the life they were leading brought strong appetites, and all fell to with the vigor of health and strength. Herbert was in fine spirits, and said he felt better than at any time since leaving home. There was little doubt that he had received wonderful benefit from his trip, and, if nothing in the way of a set back occurred, he had the best reason to believe he would be fully restored to health, long before the time came for his return home.

The Texans still avoided all reference to Rickard, and Nick decided to await a good opportunity before telling his young friend of the remarkable incident. He was resolved to ask no questions and to show no curiosity.

"I can stand it as long as they," he said to

himself, "and shall give them their own time to speak about it or leave it alone as they may prefer."

It took the party but a brief time to load up their two pack animals, and to saddle, bridle, and mount their ponies. Then, when they faced the northwest, they formed a picturesque sight.

Each of the four was mounted on a wiry pony of Spanish stock, active, intelligent, and enduring. Not one of them had ever felt the touch of currycomb or brush. Nick and Herbert, who had aimed to equip themselves as much like their adult companions as possible, were provided with ponderous saddles of wood and leather, weighing fully a dozen pounds apiece, with a pommel almost six inches in diameter. Those of the cowboys were quite costly, being sprinkled with silver stars on different parts of their surface.

Two cinches were required to hold each of the saddles in place, a forward and a flank girth. The wardrobe of the Texans has already been described, but I should have stated that the boys had imitated them in that respect also. They were provided with the broad-brimmed wool hat, known by the Mexican name of sombrero, with a jacket of ducking, shirts of calico or hickory, trousers of stout stuff, over which were worn leather leggings. All had heavy boots, to which were attached two-inch rowels, and the pack animals, besides the heavy blankets, simple cooking utensils, and various articles, carried a slicker of oiled linen for each, which, when the weather was threatening, enveloped the rider from head to heels.

There were two articles, however, carried by the cowboys which the boys did not have. Those were lariats (called in Southern California only by the name of lasso). They were about forty feet long and were composed of eight pliable rawhide thongs, plaited into ropes of a half-inch diameter. Strubell and Lattin were experts in the use of the lariat, an accomplishment which the boys could not hope to attain, since they had deferred the necessary practice until too late in life.

CHAPTER X.

DANGER IN THE EAST.

THE sun was no more than fairly above the horizon when the party were on the move, headed in the direction named. The expected norther did not come, the weather continuing as perfect as heart could wish. The uneven ground rendered the progress slow for a couple of hours, the horsemen being obliged to pick their way with care; but, by bearing to the right, better ground was reached, and they struck into an easy gallop which lasted for several hours.

"Strubell," said Herbert, who with Nick was riding beside the Texan, the other being at the rear with the pack animals, "do you expect to find any use for that lasso?"

"You mean the *lariat*," replied the cowboy, looking down at the rope coiled at his saddle; "can't say, but Baker and I make it a rule to go prepared for business. We may strike a job in New Mexico, after taking a look at the ranch for Mr. Lord."

"But you could get them there."

"Of course, but I've used this for years, just as Baker has his, and we are so accustomed to them that we prefer to take them with us, just as you will soon grow to prefer your pony and your Winchester above all others."

"When is the harvest time, as you may call it, for cattle?" asked Nick, who was always on the lookout for a chance to increase his store of knowledge.

"The spring; that's when the big herds are put up for the drive, and that's the season too, when the yearly round-up takes place."

"What's that for?"

"To apportion the unmarked calves and yearlings among the owners of stock on the range, so they can be branded."

"I should think there would be a confusion of brands."

"No; that can never happen, for the law requires the brand to be recorded in the county clerk's office. It is generally the initials of the owner's name, with perhaps some device to help distinguish it. The county clerk sees to it that no two are the same. But," added the Texan, "the law compels every cattle owner to record also with the county clerk the ear-marks, crops, half-crops, upper and under bits, upper and under slopes, splits, swallow-forks, and jingle-bobs. When all this is done, the ranchman can identify his property as easily as you could pick out your own father in a crowd."

"Suppose a lot of branded cattle are sold?" asked Nick.

"That seller is compelled to counterbrand them, and in case they are driven from the State, the buyer is obliged to road-brand them with a device different from his regular brand, and must record it in every county through which he passes."

"I should think some of the cattle would become pretty well covered with brands."

"So they do; after a few shiftings about, I have seen them so thickly branded that there seemed no place for anything new in that line. It doesn't require many transfers to do this when the burned letters, as I have seen them, are nearly a foot long."

"How is the branding done?"

"When convenient, the animal is driven between two parallel lines of fencing, called a chute, bars being placed before and behind him. He is then helpless, and the operator does the work at his leisure. But fences (except the wire kind that the big owners are stretching across the country) are scarce, and we generally have to go to the help of the brander."

"How do you manage it?"

"Easily enough; slip about eight feet of the end of the lariat through the ring, and, putting a loop at the other end, over the pommel of the saddle, I gather the coils into my bridle hand, holding the noose in my right, and start my pony on a gallop. The animal that I want breaks into a run. I quickly get near enough to drop the noose over its head or fore feet, and the pony wheels the other way and braces himself for the shock that he knows is coming and which throws the animal to the ground. The minute he goes down, the branders seize him by the head and tail, and the hot iron does its work."

"The operation must be painful," suggested Herbert.

"Well," replied Strubell, "I suppose the animal doesn't enjoy it overmuch, but it isn't so bad as many think, for the brander must take great care not to burn through the skin into the flesh."

"What harm would be done by *that?*"

"The brand would be blotched, and a good many dishonest people would find an excuse for getting their brands mixed; but that isn't the worst trouble," added the cowboy, "for after the branding comes the blow-fly, which is the pest of Texas."

"What is his style of working?"

"He deposits his eggs under the raw sore, and, before long, thousands of screw worms are eating their way toward the vitals of the animal."

"What is done to check them?"

"We have different remedies, which only half do their work, but the best that I know of is cresylic ointment. In order to apply it, however, the animal must be roped and sometimes thrown down."

"It looks as if the cowboy has more work than play in his business," said Nick, with a laugh.

Strubell turned and stared at him a moment, as if pitying his ignorance.

"If you have any doubt about it, just try it for six months or a year. We spend most of our time in the saddle from daylight till dark. When on the trail, our diet is bacon, bread, and coffee, and not overmuch of that. I have gone twenty hours without a mouthful, for the simple reason that I hadn't the time to ride to the cook wagon to get it. When one pony gave out, I jumped on another and rode him like a house afire."

"What was the cause for such hard work?"

"Chiefly stampedes, which set the animals wild. When following the Old Cattle Trail, northward through Texas and Kansas, I have had five thousand cattle scattered to every point of the compass by a thunder-storm, despite all we could do to keep them together. Sometimes they become crazy for water, start bellowing on a full run, and crowd into the first stream so fast that a hundred or two are drowned; then, when the night is still and no air stirring, nor the slightest cause, so far as you can see, exists for alarm, something will set them off again. The only explanation that I could ever think of was that the animals are troubled now and then with bad dreams, and by their cavorting frighten the others out of their wits."

"They must be guarded carefully at night?"

"Certainly; our men are divided into three reliefs, which makes it a little harder than we have it now. When the stampede breaks out, the riders have no let up night or day till the cattle are brought together again. Then, too, the Kiowas or Comanches may take it into their heads to try a little cattle speculation. They are all fine horsemen and rifle-shots, and a half dozen of the scamps can make things as lively on a dark night as a nest of hornets. However, we like it for all that," said the Texan, "because it's the only business we know; but these big cattle owners, that are fencing in most of Texas with their barbed wire, will soon take it away from us."

At this juncture, Lattin touched his pony with his spur, and placed him alongside the others.

"I wish," said he, "that you would p'int that machine of yours off there to the east, and let us know what you make of it."

His outstretched arm showed the direction named, and his friends naturally turned their attention toward that point of the compass. They were on the plain, where the grass grew plentifully, the hilly portions being in sight several miles to their left.

Before the field glass was called into use, all saw, seemingly in the very rim of the horizon, several horsemen moving apparently over a course parallel with their own, since Lattin said they had been in sight for nearly an hour, and were neither more nor less distinct than when first observed.

The glasses were passed from one to the other, and the parties were closely studied. The instruments were of great help, giving to our friends a knowledge which otherwise they could not have obtained.

All agreed that there were three horsemen,

and that one, possibly two, were white men. The third might have belonged to the same race, but, for some cause, the Texans declared that he was a half-breed, known as Jim-John, one of the worst rogues in the Southwest.

"If you know *him*," said Nick, "you ought to know the others."

"So I do," quietly replied Strubell; "one is Bell Rickard, that you introduced to us last night. They're a bad lot, and we're bound to have trouble with them before morning."

Little did the sagacious Texan suspect the startling manner in which his words were to be verified.

CHAPTER XI.

STRANGE PROCEEDINGS.

THE elder Texan turned to the boys and said:

"I must ask you to excuse Baker and me for a few minutes, while we discuss a little private business."

It was a singular request, but Nick and Herbert nodded their heads. Striking their ponies into a quick gallop, the cowboys rode a hundred yards or so in advance, before bringing their animals down to a walk. The gait of the youths was the same.

The remark made by Strubell concerning Rickard, caused Herbert to ask what it meant. Nick told him the story, adding:

"They are talking now about him and the others: look at them!"

The Texans were certainly discussing some subject with great earnestness. Inasmuch as they kept glancing to the eastward, gesticulating and often pointing in that direction, there was little doubt that Nick was right in his surmise as to the theme of their conversation.

"I wonder what it can be," said Herbert, after watching the couple, who modulated their voices so that not a word could be recognized; "it seems strange that they should treat the horse thief as a friend, when they know him to be an enemy."

"Well, I have been trying to figure it out; I supposed they would make it clear to me, but though I heard them speak about it to each other this morning, they took care not to give me a word in the way of explanation. I shall not ask them, though I was never more curious to learn anything in all my life."

"It can't be that Strubell and Lattin are on friendly terms with Rickard?" suggested Herbert.

"I might think so, after what we have just seen, though it seems cruel to suspect them of anything like that. Mr. Lord has known them for years, and says two more honest men never lived."

"You are brighter than I am, Nick; what is *your* theory?"

"Well, it is clear that Strubell and Lattin had the choice of shooting down Rickard when I drove him into camp, or of letting him go. They knew it was of no use to ask a pledge of him in payment for their kindness, for he wouldn't regard any promise as binding; so, not willing to treat him as he deserved, perhaps they took the fellow for what he was, and then let him go."

"You may be right, but the explanation doesn't amount to much, and doesn't satisfy me."

"Nor me either. I would like to hear yours."

"I haven't any. They are hard at it now!"

The Texans were talking more excitedly than ever, but did not forget to keep their voices so low that no stray word reached the ears of the puzzled youths.

The conference, however, speedily reached its conclusion. Their talking ceased, and, bringing their horses to a standstill, they waited for the boys and the pack horses to join them.

The faces of Strubell and Lattin showed signs of the stirring conversation, but, as the boys anticipated, they were silent as to the theme.

"We must make a change in our course," said the elder, who immediately turned the head of his pony to the westward, in the direction of the hills among which they had spent the previous night. It was near noon, and the major part of the day was gone, when they reached the rougher section where the Texans said the camp was to be made.

They showed their usual good judgment in the selection of a favorable site, for it was near another running stream, larger than the previous one, though the current was roiled and lukewarm. They might count themselves fortunate, however, that they were able to find water at all; for thirst has caused the death of untold thousands of cattle on the vast plains of Texas, and brought great suffering to those who have ventured not alone upon the Llano Estacado, but in other localities where moisture is almost unknown.

The pack horses were unloaded, saddles and bridles removed, and the ponies allowed to crop the scanty grass. It was too early for the regular evening meal, but considerable fuel was gathered; and, much sooner than there seemed to be any need for it, a fire was started, the smoke from which rose vertically, and was of so dark a color that it must have been visible for a long distance across the plain.

During all this time the three horsemen in the eastern horizon were not forgotten. The glasses were often turned thither, and there could be no doubt that Rickard and his companions were keeping our friends in sight. Evidently they were determined that they should not be lost.

The use of spy glasses has never been common among the cowmen, who are generally gifted with such keen eyesight that they scorn everything in the nature of artificial help. Counting upon this fact, it was not unlikely that Rickard believed that, by hovering on the line of invisibility, he would escape attention, or at least suspicion, on the part of the

Texans. Had he known of the field glasses, he must have made an important change in his programme.

The fact that our friends were without a particle of food did not cause them concern. They were not likely to suffer from starvation, for, beside the stray cattle that they were warranted in using in an emergency (always holding themselves ready to reimburse the owner when it could be done), there were antelope and other animals to be found among the hills.

But Lattin stated that, unless some kind of game would be accommodating enough to come forward and offer itself as a sacrifice to their needs, they would content themselves with a good cup of coffee around, making up for the light meal when morning should come.

When the sun sank behind the hills, Rickard and his party became invisible to the naked eye. The supposition might have been that they had withdrawn and would be seen no more, but for the story told by the field glasses. Under their power it was discovered that the scamps had dismounted near a small arroya or natural depression, and compelled their animals to lie down. Seating themselves at the same time on the grass, they filled too small an angle for the unassisted eye to note them across the intervening space.

Strubell turned to Lattin and spoke:

"Bell's cunning, but he does not dream about the spy glasses."

"We're bound to hear from him before morning," replied Lattin.

They did not mean that their words should be overheard, but Nick caught them all, though he affected ignorance.

The next sentences were meant for the youths.

"Hadn't we better move over the trail into the hills, Ard?" asked the younger Texan, as though the idea had just come to him.

"Why should we do that?" inquired the other, as if in surprise.

"Well, you know of that spring where we've camped many a time, and once had the brush with half a hundred Comanches. There are more rocks and bowlders there, and everything is a blamed sight better for a fight than it is here."

"Now, Baker, you aint so foolish as to think Bell and the others mean to disturb us?" asked Strubell, apparently forgetting the words uttered by himself only a few minutes before.

"Well, maybe not, but you know as well as me that it won't do to trust him further than you can see him."

"I tell you, Baker, what will be better," spoke up Strubell, like a man with a new and brilliant idea; "we'll send the boys ahead to the spring with the pack horses, while we wait here and find out just what Bell is up to."

"That is a good plan," added Lattin heartily; "let's do it."

The Texans now turned to Nick and Herbert, as though they did not suspect they had caught any of the conversation.

"Boys, we want to watch Bell and the others for a while, and have made up our minds to let you ride some distance over the trail, while we stay here and watch. I have proposed it, and Baker agrees that the plan is a good one. You have no objections?"

It occurred to Nick to ask in what way it was likely to improve their eyesight and the power of the glasses, by sending him and Herbert off. Surely their presence or absence could not operate one way or the other. The proposition was not very profound or bright, but, keeping back his thoughts, he promptly answered:

"Herbert and I are always ready to do cheerfully whatever you decide is best for us."

"Thanks!—spoken like a man. Now, you see the trail just beyond," added Strubell, pointing to a faintly marked path; "it has been used since the days of old Moses Austin and Sam Houston, and is so plain that you can't miss it. It leads into the hills for a quarter of a mile, and then turns north through a sort of valley. A little more than half a mile further, and you will come upon one of the prettiest springs of water in Texas. There's where you will unsaddle and make camp for to-night."

"When will you join us?"

"We hope to do so in the course of a few hours, but don't be alarmed if you see nothing of us before morning."

CHAPTER XII.

WHAT DOES IT MEAN?

BEFORE parting with the Texans, Nick Ribsam handed his field glass to Strubell, with the remark that he and Lattin would be likely to find it of use, and it could be well spared, since Herbert had one of his own. The coffee was prepared before the breaking up took place, for the cooking utensils were to go with the boys, and the men did not expect to have much leisure for preparing the delicious refreshment.

The trail, to which several references have been made, showed no evidence of having been recently travelled, though, in the course of time, a great many animals must have found their way through the hills by that route, which Nick took, with the pack horses stringing after, and Herbert bringing up the rear.

It was too strait to admit of two horsemen riding abreast, and there were places where there was none too much room for a single animal. The path wound in and out among and around bowlders and large rocks, with stunted vegetation here and there, all the time steadily ascending, until a height of several hundred feet was attained, beyond which the descent was gradual, until the same level was reached on the other side.

The distance across the ridge or small mountain spur has been named—about one-fourth of a mile. It is probable that it was first made by the feet of wild animals when they were more numerous in the neighborhood, and was afterward used by Indians and hunters in passing to and fro through that portion of Texas. It was not the first time that the speechless part of creation has blazed the path for the pioneer to follow after them.

Nick Ribsam, having placed himself at the head of the little party, started his pony, Jack, on a moderate walk, the others following at the same pace, with Herbert and his Jill at the rear. They had named their animals that day, and both were surprised at the intelligence, speed, and endurance they developed.

It was impossible for the boys not to form a fondness for the ponies, since they were so worthy, and showed a strong affection for their masters.

The sun was well above the horizon, and the youths had plenty of time at command. At the highest portion of the path, where the space was broad enough for a dozen animals to stand side by side, the boys came together.

"I guess," said Nick, from his saddle to Herbert on his right, "that you understand what all this means."

"I suspect," replied the elder, "that Strubell and Lattin are preparing for a fight with Rickard and his men."

"I've no doubt that's it, and they want us out of the way; they are pretty shrewd fellows, but I can't help wondering what answer Strubell would have made, if I had asked him how our absence would be likely to help him and Lattin better than our presence. Well, no doubt they have good reason to want us beyond gunshot; we couldn't give them any help, and might prove a hindrance, and they think too much of us to allow us to run into danger when they can prevent it."

"Nick," said Herbert, as if giving expression to a thought that had been in his mind for some time; "I wish I could think as you do about things, but I can't."

The younger lad looked at him with surprise.

"What's the odds, if we don't see everything in exactly the same light? But I am not sure that I understand you."

"Let's dismount for a few minutes."

The open space where the four animals were standing was so walled in by masses and piles of stone and vegetation that, although considerably higher than their friends at the foot of the ridge, the latter were invisible. By climbing a large, irregular bowlder, the Texans were in plain sight.

"Don't let them see us," said Herbert, "but let's watch them for a while: maybe you can explain things, and maybe you can't."

Nick was a little disturbed by the words of Herbert, though it should be stated that it was not the mind of either to suspect the Texans of anything but the truest friendship toward them; but it looked very much as if something was on foot which they wished to keep secret from their younger companions.

Strubell and Lattin were standing beside each other, with their whole attention directed eastward, where Rickard and his companions were known to be. At the moment the boys observed them, the elder Texan was holding the field glass levelled, while Lattin was doing what he could in the way of observation by shading his eyes with one hand. They were too far off to learn whether any words passed between the cowboys.

"I don't notice anything to cause question," remarked Nick, after viewing the couple for several minutes. "They are simply studying the horse thieves over yonder, in the hope of finding out something about their purposes. We have been doing the same thing, off and on, for a number of hours."

"And you think there will be a fight?"

"It looks that way; it seems to me that Strubell and Lattin are satisfied that those fellows yonder are bent on stealing our horses, and that they are likely to hang to us for days and nights, in the hope of getting a good chance to do so. So our friends have made up their minds that the best thing is to settle it at once, and by sending us off they have cleared the deck for action."

"You put it very well," said Herbert, whose admiration of his companion's brightness never grew less; "and maybe, since you have explained some things so well, you will tell us about others."

The youths now took turns in studying the group across the plain. The sun was out of sight behind the hills to their rear, but the eastern horizon, being relieved from the glare, was more favorable than before for observation through the instrument.

The three horses of the rogues were seen to be on their feet, with their riders standing beside them, as if about to climb into the saddles. One of the company, evidently Rickard himself, was several paces in advance of the others, as motionless as a statue, and evidently staring in turn toward the Texans at the foot of the ridge.

"It looks to me," said Nick, passing the glass back to Herbert, "as though he is using a field glass: can it be possible?"

"What is there so wonderful about that? The cowboys may not be fond of spy glasses, but it would be strange if some of them did not employ all the help they could get in their business."

Ceasing the conversation for the moment, the boys gave their whole attention to seeing what they could see.

Lattin, having passed the glass to Strubell, stepped back to where the fire was beginning to burn low, and threw on a few sticks. When the ascending smoke increased in volume, he took off his broad-brimmed hat and waved it in an odd way over the blaze. The result was that the volume of smoke, instead of ascending vertically, was broken into what might be called a regular irregularity, the appearance being peculiar and different from anything the the youths had ever observed before.

"That's a signal to the horse thieves," said Herbert, "and I would give a good deal to know what it means."

"So would I," added Nick, more disturbed by the sight than he was willing to admit.

It looked as if Herbert was right, but, if so, the singular feature of the business was that all the signalling seemed to be done by Strubell and Lattin. Nothing, so far as could be perceived, was sent in response by Rickard.

If there were actual communication going on between the parties, it was beyond the power of Nick and Herbert to frame a satisfactory explanation. Why intercourse should be held at such long range, when seemingly there was no reason for the mutual playing off, was a problem beyond ordinary acuteness.

But while the two were speculating, Herbert, with his field glass to his eye, began sweeping every part of the visible horizon. He had no special object in doing this, but thought he might perceive other horsemen, who had nothing to do with their friends or enemies.

Suddenly he startled Nick by an exclamation.

"Follow the direction of my finger!" he said, "and tell me what you see."

He pointed almost north, that is in a line parallel with the ridge which they were crossing; and, without the aid of the field glass, Nick observed a second column of smoke of precisely the same appearance as that produced by Baker Lattin at the foot of the hills.

Apparently it was a mile distant, its location being at one corner of a right-angled triangle, with the horse thieves and Texans at the other two respective corners. The course of the ridge shut Strubell and Lattin from the sight of those that were managing the second fire. The parties could not have caught the first mutual glimpse, and yet nothing was more reasonable to believe than that they were telegraphing important messages back and forth to each other.

CHAPTER XIII.

AN UNEXPECTED SIGNAL.

THE mystery to the lads was deeper than ever. Matters were inexplainable before, and now they were still more involved.

"It strikes me," said Herbert, "that the best course for us is to stay where we are and watch things."

"Nothing would suit me better, and yet it would be hardly right, after our promise to Strubell and Lattin. They asked us to ride forward to the spring, and we promised to do so. If we stay here we break our word. True, we would be sure to pick up some interesting information, but it would be of a kind that they don't want us to have, at least for the present."

"You are right, as you always are," replied Herbert; "it did not occur to me in that light; let us go on."

Walking back to where their ponies were waiting, they remounted and started forward in the same order as before. Both were busy with their thoughts, and filled with a disquiet which disturbed them a good deal. They would have been glad to drive away the misgivings, but could not. The conviction was strong on each that a grave crisis was at hand, and that, before the setting sun showed itself again, every member of the party was likely to become involved in greater peril than they had faced since their union.

The trail continued descending at the moderate rate of its ascent, and, at the point named by the Texans, it turned sharply northward, following a course parallel to the ridge and at its base.

They expected to travel about a half mile over the new course, which they found freer from bowlders and obstructions than before. The horses moved with a brisker pace, as if they knew camp was not far off, and a long and grateful rest was at hand.

At the moment of emerging from the hills, and reaching the lower level, the sun dipped below the horizon and twilight began. Far to the westward stretched the broad prairie, with the faint blue line of a distant chain of mountains, resting like a cloud against the clear sky beyond.

The sweep of the field glass failed to reveal any living creature. It seemed to the youths as if they were entering upon a vast solitude, where they were the only intruders. They pushed along the path in silence, the sounds of their animals' hoofs being all that broke the solemn stillness. Nick turned his head now and then, and, looking over the backs of the pack horses, saw that Herbert was more thoughtful than usual. His face wore a grave expression, which proved that the situation oppressed him.

"But," added Nick to himself, "suppose his suspicions are right, what harm can result? If Strubell and Lattin are friends of Rickard, and have an understanding with him, in what way can it affect us? Mr. Lord may be deceived into believing they are honest, but we have nothing to fear. None of them has ill designs against us, and, whatever the relations of the parties, our friends would never permit the outlaws to molest us."

Nick might have persuaded himself fully to this faith, but for the remembrance of the scene the night before. He could not forget the threat of Rickard as he walked off in the gloom, nor would that bad man forgive the indignity put upon him by a boy in the presence of a couple of acquaintances. Such characters are as revengeful as American Indians, and he would lose no opportunity of paying him therefor. It is a sad fact that about half the world are engaged in "getting even" with the other half, for fancied wrongs received at their hands.

Nick had not ridden far when he abruptly checked his pony and called to Herbert:

"Halloo! here's something we didn't bargain for."

"What's that?" asked the surprised Herbert.

"Come forward and see."

The elder was about to dismount, when he perceived that, by crowding, he could force Jill alongside of his friend. He did so, and discovered that which had checked the procession.

The trail which they had been following divided, one branch turning to the right and the other to the left. The divergence was so slight, that there could not be much space between the two at a considerable distance beyond, unless the angle increased.

"It's singular that neither Strubell nor Lattin said anything about this," remarked Nick, looking inquiringly at Herbert, who was following the path with his eye.

"I don't understand that any more than I understand the other matters we have been talking about. How are we going to tell which is the right course?"

It will be remembered that the youths had been riding northward, along the base of the ridge, where the ground was comparatively level; but for some distance the trail turned slightly in among the hills, compelling a moderate descent, and a more winding course, through and around the bowlders and obstructions. At the point where Nick had reined up his pony this trend became more pronounced, while the path on the left led down toward the foot of the hills.

The difficulty lay in the fact that each was marked with equal distinctness, and it was, therefore, beyond their power to decide with certainty which was the right one to follow. This was proven when Nick gave it as his belief that the one on the right was the main trail, while Herbert was equally positive that the reverse was the case; how, therefore, was the question to be settled?

"There's one thing clear to me," said Nick, seeing how matters stood; "Strubell and Lattin are certain that we are not placing ourselves in any danger by leaving them behind and riding on alone; for we agree that the movement was meant for our good. We haven't caught the first sight of man or animal, so we need not be troubled. Now, I will follow the upper path, which I think is the right one, while you take the lower. That will be better than for each of us to take the wrong course, and then come back to travel the same distance along the right one."

"But how will we manage it?" asked Herbert, who was not well pleased with the proposal, despite his confidence in Nick's judgment.

"In the first place, we shall not be far apart after going a long way, unless there is a more abrupt divergence than we see here. If I reach the spring, as I feel sure I shall, I will call to you and you can join me."

"By riding back here to this fork—what will I gain by that?"

"I think you can save considerable distance by riding across the intervening ground, though, if that can't be done, and you have to double on your own trail, it will be but one, instead of two, who has to do it. If we keep together, and both go wrong, we will have double work, while by dividing, one is as sure to be right as the other is to go astray; consequently half the labor will be saved."

"What about the pack horses?"

"I guess they would better go with me."

Herbert laughed.

"That shows your faith in your own theory, but I am willing, though just as sure as you, that you are putting extra duty on the animals."

"When I strike the spring," continued Nick, with a smile, "I will give a whistle, which you will understand as a call for you, and you can cut across lots or gallop back to this point and follow after me."

"At any rate," added Herbert, "I don't see that the matter is very important, for we shall not be separated long. I will whistle to you when I reach the spring. Since I have only Jill, I will press on faster than you, and save you extra work."

With this laughing parting, each set out to verify his own theory, confident that they would soon come together again.

Nick was inclined to force his pony into a gallop, for the trail was so free from obstructions that this could have been easily done, but he was afraid it would disorganize the pack horses. Their loads were not heavy and were generally fixed so securely in place that they could gallop whenever required, without risk to the property ; but the goods had been hastily adjusted, when on the other side of the ridge, and were likely to become disarranged, for the animals were so trained to follow their leader that when he increased his pace they were quite sure to do the same.

"I knew I was right!" exclaimed Nick, with a laugh, after riding a fourth of a mile, as he came upon a broad, deep, crystalline spring, which warranted all the praise the Texans had bestowed on it; "I don't see why Herbert was so positive; I've got him this time, and he'll have to own up."

As agreed upon, he placed the tip of his finger and thumb against his tongue to emit the signal; but, before he could do so, the very same call reached him from the foot of the hills. Herbert had summoned him to retrace his steps to the fork and join him!

"What under the sun can *that* mean?" asked the amazed Nick, holding his thumb and finger in front of his mouth, undecided what to do.

CHAPTER XIV.

A STRANGE ABSENCE.

NICK RIBSAM might well be puzzled. Just ahead and on his right was the most enchanting natural spring of water that he had ever beheld. It was circular in shape, fully two yards in diameter and ten or twelve inches deep in the middle. From several places on the bottom the water bubbled up in a way that tumbled the sand in miniature fountains, which hid the current flinging the particles upward from below.

This basin was so clear that at first sight one was doubtful whether there was any water there at all; but the bubbling sand and the vigorous stream flowing away and across the trail, and losing itself among the rocks and vegetation, removed all question on that point.

The spring was partly shaded by a black bowlder leaning so far over that it seemed on the point of tumbling in, while the scene in the immediate vicinity was rougher than any through which they had passed since crossing the ridge.

Domestic as well as wild animals are quick to discern the presence of water, and Nick had seen proof in the actions of Jack that he knew he was near the spring, some time before he himself knew it. The three were so pleased that they hastened their pace, and crowded their noses into the cool element, of which they drank with an enjoyment beyond description.

The youth meant to have a deep refreshing draught himself, but he had not the heart to check the ponies. He could wait better than they; they were not unclean animals, and the spring would quickly free itself of all traces of the contact with their silken noses.

But while Jack was stretching his head downward and standing with one fore leg bent at the knee, the better to reach the water, his rider prepared to give the call for Herbert to join him, when he was taken all aback by catching precisely the same signal from his friend.

There could be no mistake about it: he had heard it too often to confound it with any other sound.

He had noticed, while riding along the trail, that the divergence became more pronounced, thus separating him from Herbert by a greater distance than he had anticipated. As nearly as he could judge from the whistle, his friend was nearly, if not quite an eighth of a mile away, and between them the slope was so filled with rocks, bowlders, and stunted vegetation that travelling with a horse was out of the question. A trained mountaineer would find the task anything but an easy one. Herbert, therefore, must turn squarely about, and ride back to the fork in the trail, thus travelling double the distance made by Nick and the pack horses.

A moment's reflection convinced the latter that Herbert had made a natural mistake. The stream, winding its way in that direction, probably formed a pool near the other part, so large and clear and beautiful that the youth mistook it for the spring itself.

"But he will see his error," reflected Nick,

sending out the ringing blast by which he had summoned his friend many a time; "he doesn't like to own up, but, when he looks upon this, he can't help himself."

Nick was convinced that there were few such natural springs in that section of Texas, though similar ones are found in plenty further east and among some of the mountainous portions.

The horses having had their fill, stepped back, and Nick began his preparations for spending the night. Everything was taken from the backs and heads of the animals and placed in a pile on the ground near at hand, while they were left to crop the grass, which was green and quite luxuriant in the vicinity of the stream.

By the time everything was complete, darkness had come. The animals were not tethered, for there was little to be feared of their running away, unless interfered with by outsiders, of which no one dreamed.

Nick now began to look for the coming of Herbert. Both paths were so easily travelled that he ought to appear in the course of twenty minutes, and a full half hour had gone by.

"I wonder whether anything could have happened to him," said Nick, gazing down the trail in the gathering gloom, and feeling a renewal of the fears that troubled him so much in the afternoon.

He once more whistled with the power of a steam engine, and paused for the response. It was impossible, as he had learned long before, that Herbert should have made his way on horseback across the space separating the trails, and he, therefore, gave his attention to the route over which he himself had just travelled.

Nothing was to be seen of his friend, and the suspicion came to Nick that possibly he was pouting because of his mistake, but the thought was dismissed the next minute as unworthy of Herbert, who, if disposed in that direction, was in no mood to do so at the present time.

"But where can he be?" repeated Nick, recalling the preceding winter, when he went astray in the pursuit of the second moose and caused himself and Pierre Ardeau no end of worriment of mind. As the darkness increased, Nick Ribsam became aware of another discomforting fact. The wind was beginning to blow, and the cold was rapidly increasing. The norther prophesied by the Texans was at hand.

This being evident, he quickly prepared for it. He had gathered a quantity of limbs and twigs, but they were unlighted, he intending to await the arrival of his friend Herbert; but he now started the fire as quickly as possible, for, aside from its needed warmth, it would do much to dispel the gloom oppressing him.

Few who have not experienced a Texan norther can understand their fierce suddenness. I was once riding in a stage in the southern part of the State, the day was mild and balmy, and a middle-aged gentleman from New York sat in the seat with me. His overcoat was in his trunk, which was strapped at the rear of the stage. We were talking, when all at once a norther came howling across the country. My friend shouted to the driver to unstrap his trunk, so as to allow him to unlock it. The driver promptly obeyed, the gentleman leaping out of the vehicle, hastily unfastening his luggage, and bringing out the extra garment. Only a few minutes were occupied, and yet his teeth were chattering and he was shivering and blue with cold while hurriedly donning his greatcoat.

A young man in Dallas told me he was standing on the opposite side of the street in his shirt sleeves; a norther arrived; he struck diagonally for his home on a dead run; that home was less than two blocks off; he insisted that if he had been delayed on the way by so much as a fall he would have frozen to death; but, somehow or other, I think he exaggerated things.

But by the time Nick Ribsam had the fire going, he was shivering. He gathered his heavy blanket closely about him and sat down near the blaze, but was still cold. The ponies felt it. They shrunk against the rocks and wherever they could find any shelter, and looked dismal and wretched. No blankets had been provided for them, but the luggage of the entire party was at command and Nick's

9

sympathy led him to appropriate the articles without a moment's hesitation. It was a kind act and did much for the comfort of the dumb beasts.

What about Strubell and Lattin? They must suffer, but they were acclimated and would find some means of warding off the full effort of the cutting winds, without the help of extra clothing.

But poor Herbert! Nick fairly gasped as he thought of him. He was in his ordinary costume, and of course had not started a fire. He would not be likely to do so, since he was on his way to join Nick and would depend on him for everything of that sort.

"Heaven save him," prayed Nick, "but if he doesn't arrive soon he must perish. *Hurry, Herbert!*" he called at the top of his voice.

In his anxiety, Nick started down the path with the extra blanket flung over his arm, while he was so swathed in his own that he resembled an Indian chief, striding along the trail.

Night had fully come, and the sky, which had been quite clear during most of the day, was overcast, so that he could see but a short distance in any direction. Still he hurried on, confident every minute that the forms of Herbert and Jill would loom to view in the darkness.

But rod after rod was passed, and they did not appear. Suddenly Nick stooped down and placed his ear against the earth.

"I hear his pony's hoofs!" he exclaimed, raising his head and peering forward, "but why is he so long on the way?"

Applying his ear again, the startling fact was evident: the sound of the horse's hoofs was fainter than before. The animal was receding instead of approaching.

"Something has gone wrong with the poor fellow, and what can I do to help him?"

CHAPTER XV.

CAUGHT FOUL.

NICK RIBSAM was partly right in his supposition about his missing friend, Herbert Watrous.

That young gentleman rode along the lower trail, as confident as anyone could be that he was right and Nick was wrong. He did not press Jill, for the pony had done considerable hard riding during the day, but he arrived at the end of his brief journey a little in advance of the other.

"I knew it," he said at the moment of catching sight of the pool of clear water, which, like the spring, was slightly to the right of the path; "there aren't many brighter boys than Nick, but he makes his mistake once in a while, like other folks."

And then, as his pony walked forward to drink, his rider gave out the signal intended to summon Nick to the spot.

CAUGHT FOUL. 133

"He will feel cheap when he finds he is wrong, but he is manly enough to own up to it, and admit that some folks know——"

Sitting astride of his animal while he was helping himself to a drink, Herbert made good use of his eyes. Just then he observed that, though the pool resembled a natural spring, it was not. It was fed by a stream pouring into the upper portion, as large as that which formed the outlet, while there was no bubbling from the bottom.

"Whew!" whistled the astonished youth; "it begins to look as if it wasn't Nick that had made a slip—hello!"

At that moment the call came ringing down from the upper trail. The matter was settled. Nick had struck the right spot, and all Herbert could do was to ride back along the path to the fork and join him.

He was on the point of starting back, when it occurred to him that it might be possible to shorten the distance by cutting across the neck of land, as talked about before they parted. The promise of being able to do so looked more encouraging from below than above.

Slipping down from the saddle, Herbert began picking his way through the rough portion, and advanced several rods before reaching a section where a horse would find the travelling difficult.

"He could make his way this far easily enough," he said, halting and looking back, "but it doesn't seem so easy further on."

He advanced more carefully, for he was beginning to doubt the feasibility of the plan. It will be readily seen that while he was so uncertain as to the best course, he was consuming more time than he suspected. Night was rapidly closing in, and he was still debating what was best to do, when he noticed the increasing cold.

"It's the norther, sure enough!" he exclaimed, starting back to mount his horse; "a little late, but it's getting there all the same."

In fact it "got there" with such emphasis that, before Herbert could force his way to the pool of water, he thought he would freeze to death. There was no need of answering the signal of Nick, and, catching sight of the outlines of what seemed a mass of rocks in the darkness, he made for them, intent only on securing shelter for the moment, or until the cutting wind abated enough to allow him to venture out to recover his horse.

Meanwhile, the latter, who had had more than one previous experience with northers, was trying to help himself somewhat after the same fashion as his master. Since the arctic breath from the distant Rocky Mountains came from the north, Jill began edging away from it by taking the back trail, just as cattle drift before a long continued and violent storm of sleet and snow.

It must not be supposed that the pony held any purpose of deserting his master. He had never tried to do anything of the kind, and it would be injustice to accuse him in the present instance; but the instinct of self-preservation was as strong in him as in any other animal, and he saw no other way of lessening his sufferings than by edging along the back trail.

When he reached the fork where the two paths separated, he may have recalled his situation and he may not. Be that as it may, it was too much to expect him to face about and advance in the teeth of the norther, before which he had retreated so far, unless he was compelled to do so. No one was there to urge him with spur, and instead, therefore, of turning his course, he kept on.

He had moved so reluctantly to this point that he did not reach it until Nick Ribsam knelt down a short distance off and put his ear to the ground. By this time, too, it probably struck Jill that he was moving more slowly than was wise. He therefore struck a quicker gait, speedily passing beyond hearing in the gloom, and leaving Nick puzzled, mystified, and anxious beyond expression.

All this time, Herbert Watrous never dreamed that his pony was steadily increasing the distance between them. If he had known it, he could have taken no steps to prevent the mishap, for his whole mental and physical energies were bent toward saving himself from perishing with the fearful cold.

Nothing could have been more fortunate than his finding a small cavern. It was really providential that he should stumble upon it, and he would have fared ill had he failed to do so. It was of slight extent, being no more than a dozen feet in depth, and of such narrow compass that he bumped his head or struck his limbs against the sides at every movement he made.

Crouching in the furthest corner, he huddled himself together as best he could, and concluded there was hope of seeing the thing through, provided it got no worse.

"If it drops another degree, I'm a goner!" he muttered, as well as he could between his chattering teeth. "I don't see what's the use of having such weather as this in Texas, when we can get all we want at the North Pole. It beats anything I ever heard of in Maine; I'm glad Nick has the blankets, for he must need them."

For fully two hours Herbert shrank in his place, in the cavity among the rocks. During most of that time, the wind moaned around the front, as if seeking him out that it might freeze his very marrow. The hardest thing for him was to comprehend that he was actually in Texas, where but a brief while before the temperature was like a poet's dream.

There was one thing, however, which he comprehended very clearly. If he stayed where he was much longer, he would never come out alive. He had not heard the second signal of Nick, but was confident that he was able to take care of himself, with his almost unlimited supply of blankets.

There was one way of warming himself: that was by vigorous exercise. That might not answer perfectly, but it must help matters. He, therefore, crept out of his refuge, and began making his way down to the pool near which he had left his pony. The gloom was too profound for him to see anything distinctly, and he came within a hair of pitching headlong into the water, along the edges of which a thin coating of ice had formed.

It was at this time that Herbert was gratified to notice a decided rising of the temperature. The relief was great, but not enough wholly to relieve his sufferings. He called his pony by name, but of course there was no response.

"He has been more sensible than me," he

concluded, "for he has gone to the spring, where Nick has started a fire for him and made them all comfortable while I suffered."

The reader need not be reminded that once again Herbert was off in his reckoning.

He spent the next ten minutes in jumping about, swinging his arms, and going through the most violent gymnastics possible. The effect was good. His benumbed limbs became supple, the chilled surface began glowing, and a grateful warmth crept through his entire system.

It would have been folly to try to reach Nick by working across the neck of bowlders and obstructions, and he started down the trail in the direction taken by Jill, though he was a long way behind him.

This required no little care, even though he was following a distinctly marked trail. In the darkness he received several severe bruises, besides tumbling flat on his face more than once. But he kept his wits about him, and made sure that he did not pass the fork, where it was necessary to turn off and follow the trail taken by Nick, and which had proven to be the right one.

Here it was necessary to use still greater care than before, for the route was strange to him, and might contain dangerous pitfalls.

"Nick will wonder what's become of me," he reflected, maintaining as lively a pace as he dared, "but I hope he hasn't worried—halloo! that's good!" he added, as he caught the twinkle of a fire; "that's where I will find the good fellow, who has known enough to take care of himself and the ponies, and would have done the same with me if I hadn't been so foolish."

CHAPTER XVI.

AN ASTOUNDING DISCOVERY.

HERBERT noticed, as he went forward, that the fire was sinking so low as to show that it had not been looked after for some time. Backed against a bowlder near the spring, it was well protected from the wind, but had been fanned into a blaze that must have diffused a good deal of warmth in all directions.

The first mild surprise came to the youth when, on coming close to the smouldering camp fire, he failed to see Nick. He expected to find him resting comfortably near at hand, swathed in one of the thick blankets capable of shutting out every kind of cold except that of a norther, which will force its way through almost anything.

Stepping forward into the light of the fire, Herbert looked inquiringly around in the gloom, and called the name of his friend, repeating it several times with increasing loudness, but with no more result than in the first instance. Then the youth started out to investigate for himself.

The discovery that followed was startling. Not only Nick Ribsam, but his horse, the two pack animals and the pony belonging to Herbert, were missing! They were nowhere in the neighborhood.

The youth was knocked almost breathless. He came back beside the smouldering fire and tried to reason connectedly over the situation.

"This is ahead of everything yet," he said to himself; "it begins to look as if all actions are tinged with mystery. Nick and I couldn't understand why Strubell and Lattin should act as they did this afternoon, but I am not half as much mystified over that as over this. Nick and all the horses gone. What can it mean?"

"All that is left me, besides my weapon," he added with grim feeling, "is my field glass, but I don't need that to see what a fix I'm in, and yet I am more worried about Nick than myself——"

He thought he heard a footfall from the direction of the fork of the trails. Grasping his Winchester he moved silently back in the gloom, where he could not be seen by any lurking Indian or white enemy.

"It is Nick returning," was his thought, as he recognized the hoofs of an animal.

The next minute his own pony, saddled and bridled, as when he last saw him, walked forward in the firelight and uttered a faint whinny of pleasure at sight of his master.

"Heaven bless you!" was the grateful exclamation of Herbert as he met him and patted his neck; "I feared you were gone for good; but, Jill, how I wish you could talk that you might tell me all about Nick and the other horses."

To say the least, the pony had behaved himself in a singular fashion. I have told how he was driven along by the norther until he passed beyond the fork in the trails, Nick Ribsam catching the faint footfalls as he applied his ear to the ground, which told him the beast was receding.

No doubt there crept into the brain of this

sagacious animal a conviction that he was not doing precisely the right thing in wandering away from the spot where his master had left him, and where, of course, he expected to find him on his return.

In addition, the norther, that had brought about this breach of confidence, subsided to that extent that it was no hardship to face it. This subsidence, however, did not reach a degree that suited Jill until he had drifted off for a considerable while. Then he began edging backward, and, possibly because he divined the intentions of Herbert, he followed the main trail until he joined his master at the camp fire.

Among the many extraordinary incidents which attended the tour of Nick and Herbert through the Southwest, probably there was none more remarkable than the action of the pony Jill and the consequences flowing therefrom. He drifted away from the scene of several singular events and remained absent until they were finished. Then he came back, and had he been a little later or earlier, the whole face of history might have been changed

—that is, so far as it related to the youths I have named.

Having regained his pony, Herbert was as much perplexed as ever. It was an invaluable piece of good fortune thus securing his horse, for a person on the plains without a good steed is in the situation of the sailor without boat or ship on the ocean ; but he was totally at a loss how to proceed.

The most obvious course was to stay where he was until morning, or until some kind of knowledge came to him. The Texans had promised to join him and Nick by daylight and probably before, and it would not require them long to decide upon the best line to follow. If Nick had set out along the lower trail to search for him, he must have learned of his mistake before this; and, though it was curious that the friends had not met, the younger ought to return to his own camp fire whither he had summoned Herbert hours before.

The disquieting factor in the situation was the absence of the animals, and the return of his own ; for Herbert could not be expected to know all about the action of Jill in his encounter with the norther.

He soon became satisfied that a long wait was before him. Accordingly, the saddle and bridle were removed from the pony, that he might be free to crop the grass within reach, while his owner spent considerable time in gathering wood with which to keep the fire going. There was only a small supply of fuel on hand, and this work was necessary, therefore, on his part.

The weather had moderated to the extent that it was much the same as before the norther swept through the hills. The blaze was not needed, except for its aid in dispelling the oppressive gloom.

Herbert was seated near the fire, and had just looked at his watch and seen that it was past eleven o'clock, when he was alarmed by several discharges of rifles. They were dull, but loud enough to prevent any mistake as to their nature. The direction, too, was easily recognized as being from the other side of the ridge.

"Nick and I were right," he said, listening

with a rapidly beating heart; "Strubell and Lattin are having a fight with the horse thieves—there they go again!"

Two reports in rapid succession were heard, and then came a third and fourth, followed after an interval of several minutes by other dropping shots. These were noticed, now and then, during the next hour, after which, so far as Herbert could judge, everything remained still.

Beyond question, he was right in his belief that a lively scrimmage had taken place between Bell Rickard, Jim-John the half-breed, and their companion on one side, and the Texans on the other. As to the result, no one could tell who was not present, until some one of the participants was seen.

Though much disturbed by his fear that the cowboys had suffered, a certain pleasure came to Herbert at this proof of the genuine hostility between his friends and the rogues. It will be remembered that he had had troublesome misgivings in this respect. He felt there had been reason to doubt the honesty of Strubell and Lattin, and that, despite appearances, an understanding existed between them and the criminals who were following them so persistently.

The reports of the firearms disproved all this and showed beyond question that the Texans were good men, ready to defend their property and the youths with them, no matter how great the risks to themselves.

Herbert had decided to stay where he was until morning or some news of his friends reached him, and wait he did through the almost endless night. Toward daylight, he fell into a dreamful sleep, which lasted until the sun was above the horizon. Then he started up and stared around, a minute or two passing before he could recall all the incidents of the preceding night.

His horse had risen from the ground and was cropping the grass; the fire had smouldered to ashes, and the clear morning was as balmy and pleasant as its predecessor. Neither Nick nor the Texans were in sight; but, determined to find out something for himself, he hurriedly saddled and bridled his pony and galloped down the trail.

"He reined up, and raised his field-glass to his eye."

"They promised to be here before this," he said, referring to Strubell and Lattin; "and they would have kept their word, if they had the power to do so. One, and perhaps both, have been killed, or so badly wounded that they cannot leave the battle ground."

At the forks, the plain was so open to the westward that he reined up and raised his field glass to his eye. He had detected moving bodies in the distance, and the first view through the telescope showed them with great clearness.

A small party of horsemen were moving northward, their animals on a walk. While studying them closely, Herbert's attention was drawn to one in particular. He was riding on the extreme right, so that he was the nearest to him and was in plain sight.

A brief study of this figure left no doubt of the astounding fact that he was no other than the missing Nick Ribsam himself!

CHAPTER XVII.

THE SOLITARY PURSUER.

HERBERT held his field glass to his eyes for several minutes, while he carefully studied the group of horsemen out upon the plain. There were four of them, beside the two pack animals, all apparently well mounted, and the clear sunlight brought them into clear relief. Their ponies were walking slowly, not exactly north, but bearing a little to the west, so that the general direction was the same as that of our friends on their way to New Mexico.

The horseman on the right was Nick Ribsam. Although the distance was too great to distinguish his features, the presence of the pack horses settled the question and there was no mistaking his personality: it was he beyond all doubt.

"What can be the explanation of his presence with them?" was the question which the alarmed Herbert asked himself, as he lowered his glass and gazed absently in the direction, while he studied the most perplexing problem that had yet presented itself.

He was impressed by the fact that there were three horsemen besides his friend. That was the number that made up the band of Bell Rickard. What more likely than that the three with Nick were the horse thieves?

In the hours that had passed since they were seen, far out on the plains to the eastward, they possessed sufficient time to make their way through the hills to this point. Indeed, they could have done so after the sounds of firing ceased on the other side of the hills.

But this theory of necessity raised other perplexing questions. If those three men were the criminals, where were Strubell and Lattin? Where had they been, while the piece of treachery was pushed to a conclusion? Was it supposable that they had remained idle and permitted Nick's most dangerous enemy to get him in his power?

Certainly not—*provided it was in their power to prevent it.*

The inference could not be escaped by Herbert that the cowboys had been put out of the way by their enemies, and that, therefore, no further help was to be expected from them.

Other questions presented themselves, which would have puzzled a more experienced frontiersman than the young New Yorker.

He and Nick had discovered a second camp fire the afternoon before, to the northward. Who kindled that, and what was its significance? Evidently it had some connection with the Texans or the criminals, but nothing could be learned to indicate its nature.

Were the continued absence and silence of the cowboys explainable on any other theory than their own overthrow?

These questions, however, were put out of sight by the personal peril of Nick Ribsam, and the anxiety of Herbert to do something for him without delay.

His first inclination was to gallop back over the trail to the point where he left Strubell and Lattin the afternoon before, and tell them what had taken place. They were the only ones of whom aid could reasonably be expected.

But it has been shown that he feared the worst concerning them. Time was precious, and to cross the ridge and return would take a half hour, which might be fatal to any other step toward helping Nick. This fear was intensified by the discovery that the walk of the ponies to the westward had become a gallop, which was fast widening the gap between them and the ridge, where the distressed Herbert was trying to settle what he ought to do, if indeed he could do anything, for his loved friend.

"I will follow them," was the conclusion which he reached after briefly thinking over every phase of the question; "I don't know that it will do Nick any good, but it's just what *he* would do if our situations were changed."

Herbert was well aware that in making this important decision, the only possible hope— and it was slight indeed—of doing anything for Nick was by using the utmost discretion.

One might well ask what chance he could have against three veteran plainsmen, who were without principle or honor. Had Herbert himself been asked the question, he would have found it hard to answer. It may be said that something in the nature of a ransom suggested itself, though he was too wise to build much hope on that means.

The one thing clear in his mind was that he must hide his pursuit, if he could do so, from all knowledge of the abductors. If they possessed a field glass, as he believed was likely, they must have discerned him at the foot of the hills, provided the instrument was turned in that direction. Hopeful, however, that they had not done so, he drew his pony behind a sheltering rock, and held his gaze fixed on the horsemen, who maintained their gallop, which was fast taking them out of his natural field of vision.

He waited until the fluttering specks were barely perceptible to the unassisted eye, and then decided to follow the trail a little way to the southward, before wheeling to the west. He thought it less likely that he would be noticed, if he left the hills at a point removed from where he had been waiting so long, and where, had the criminals observed him, they would look for his reappearance.

He had ridden no more than a hundred yards, when, to his astonishment, he came upon the site of the strangers' last encampment. It was directly beside the trail, where there was no water, but the smouldering camp fire and the cropped grass showed that several hours had been passed there. More important than all to the solitary pursuer was the finding of the remains of an antelope that had furnished the party with a meal. The youth had not eaten food since the preceding noon, and, highly wrought as were his feelings, he was faint and in need of nourishment. Enough fragments were scattered about for him to obtain all he wanted in that line, so long as he was not over fastidious.

Since he was hungry and there was no saying when he could secure another meal, Herbert was wise in eating his fill. Then, when he swung himself into the saddle, he looked across the plain and failed to see the horsemen; but the glass, being brought into play, revealed them apparently in the very rim of the horizon.

"Ah, they have changed their course!" he exclaimed; "that looks as if they had no instrument after all and think I am beyond their sight."

It will be remembered that beyond the level stretch of country, another and loftier range of hills showed against the clear sky. The horsemen were moving toward them, and Herbert believed it was with the purpose of misleading him or anyone that undertook to follow them. True, the trail left by them was so marked that, once taken, it could be maintained without trouble to the end; but, for reasons already shown, they were warranted in considering that improbable.

The pursuer, however, decided to take no chances that he could avoid. Having started from the encampment of the preceding night, he was on their track from the beginning, and he meant to maintain it to the end.

Everyone knows how deceptive distance is in the clear air of the plains. Objects that appear but a few miles away prove to be two and three times as far. Herbert Watrous had been long enough in Texas to learn this fact. The range that he had noticed the afternoon before seemed to be within half a day's ride, but he was convinced it would require brisk traveling to reach it by sunset.

Then, too, the plan he had fixed upon forced him to keep a long way to the rear, so that, if the horsemen struck the other range by set of sun, the night would be well along before he could come up with them. There was no moon to help him, and this might interfere with his programme.

But, as may be said, he had put his hand to the plough and did not look back.

Contrary, however, to the maxim, this was an unfortunate mistake on his part; for, had he, after riding the major part of the distance, turned in his saddle and surveyed the course traversed, he would have made an important discovery, and one, too, that must have had an important bearing on the almost hopeless enterprise in which he was engaged.

But Herbert's interest was all in front. Nick Ribsam was in the power of his enemies, and possibly he could aid him, though common sense told him that the chances were as ninety-nine to one that he would end the business by putting himself in the same hole. A party of desperate men that were cunning enough to make the sagacious Nick prisoner were not likely to be annoyed by anything Herbert Watrous could do to checkmate them; but youth is ardent and hopeful, and none of these things weakened the pursuit of the New Yorker.

CHAPTER XVIII.

THE SECOND RANGE OF HILLS.

BUT while riding across the level plain, Herbert Watrous did a good deal of thinking, and strove hard to fix upon the wisest course to benefit the missing Nick.

Now, as I have intimated, nothing could be clearer than the foolhardiness of trying to outwit the criminals, or to aid his friend by his own shrewdness. They had made a prisoner of the youth, who Herbert knew was his superior in every respect, and could well afford to laugh at the utmost he essayed to do.

Without attempting to answer the many questions that presented themselves, he confined his speculation to one or two bearing directly upon the important business on which he was engaged.

Admitting that Bell Rickard, the crooked dealer in horse-flesh, had made a prisoner of

Nick Ribsam, it followed that he held no intention of doing him immediate harm. Had his anger been as deep and resentful as supposed, he would have shot him down at sight, instead of taking him on a long ride. Herbert shuddered at the thought that possibly he meant to prolong his suffering and torture, as do the American Indians in the case of their captives, and that his revenge would be carried out that evening. This theory, however, was so violent that it caused the youth less worriment than would be supposed. He could not believe that Rickard held any such shocking purpose. This brought Herbert back to his former belief that the frugal criminal was managing things with a view of forcing a ransom from the friends of his prisoner. While he saw numerous objections to the idea, he decided to act upon it. He meant to ride straight into the camp of the thieves, and demand their reason for what they had done.

If Rickard would agree to release Nick for a reasonable sum, Herbert would gladly pay it. He had considerable money with him, and, if that proved insufficient, he could give him drafts that would be honored in San Antonio, Santa Fé, or San Francisco. It will be remembered that Mr. Watrous had liberally provided for his son in this respect.

Should Rickard accept the proposition, he would still hold the whip hand, in case he chose to betray both boys; but it was idle to speculate. Time enough to face the varying conditions as they presented themselves.

By the time this decision crystallized in the mind of Herbert, the afternoon was half gone, and he had ridden a good many miles. He had seen no water, and, though he allowed Jill to rest himself by walking at times, yet he forced him to the verge of imprudence. Both he and his master were thirsty and hungry, but had to wait a convenient season before attending to their wants.

At intervals, he had raised his glass and studied the party, well in advance, but, as he was on their trail, this was not necessary, and a couple of hours passed without his doing so. He was so absorbed in his thoughts that he rode at the easy, swinging gait which Jill could maintain for a long time without fatigue, paying no attention to his surroundings.

The afternoon was far along, and he was drawing near the ridge that had seemed so near ever since starting, when he roused himself with the thought that he must keep his senses about him, and cease the speculating and daydreaming in which he had indulged so long.

His first natural act was to look ahead for the horsemen, but the unaided eye could not see them. The helpful field glass was then levelled, and he scanned the base of the hills from a point well to the south, along his front, and a considerable way to the north, but was surprised to observe nothing of them.

"They have ridden in among the hills, where they are out of sight, but that will make little difference, as long as I stick to their trail——"

He checked his utterance in dismay, for, looking down at the ground, he discovered that he was not on the track of the party at all. While rapt in a brown study, his pony had left it, and the anxious eyes which scanned the prairie on all sides failed to detect the first imprint of a horse's hoofs.

"Well, this is a pretty pass!" he exclaimed impatiently, as he reined up; "I left it to you, Jill, not doubting that you would attend to business; but, after all, it was my own fault."

Reflection, however, convinced him that the case was not so bad after all. He could not be far astray, and he decided to press on toward the hills, and gallop along their base, until he struck the missing trail.

That which caused him anxiety was the lateness of the hour. The top of the ridge already shut the sun from sight, and, ere long, night would close over the scene, so obscuring the footprints that further search must be hopeless.

It was this fact which caused him to touch his spur sharply against the side of Jill, and force him to a pace that he would not have done in his tired condition, but for the urgency of the case.

Jill responded gamely to the demand,

galloping with a speed that caused the still wind to whistle by the rider's face. The hills were so close that a half hour carried him to the base, and he once more brought the animal down to a walk.

It was now a question whether he was too far north or too far to the south of the point of entrance by the party in advance. If he should err, there was not enough daylight remaining to correct the mistake; he would of necessity be forced to wait until morning before going on.

Since he had to guess at it, he acted on the theory that he had struck the ridge to the south. He therefore wheeled his pony to the right, and touched him into a leisurely canter, while he kept his eyes fixed on the ground, as it swept under the hoofs of the animal.

It was certainly remarkable that Herbert's thoughts remained so fixed upon what was in front that he gave little or no attention to the rear. Once, it is true, he glanced back over the long space ridden during the day, and noted that the ridge, which had been the scene of his stirring experience of the previous night, was fast fading from sight; but the survey was so brief and hasty that it failed to take in an important feature in which he was directly concerned.

Better fortune attended his search than he anticipated, for he had ridden only a little way when he struck the footprints of the horses. It was still so light that he could readily detect them without dismounting, but that there should be no mistake, he slipped from the saddle, and, holding the bridle in one hand, walked several rods, carefully studying the marks in the earth.

He was right. It was easy to see that six horses had passed that way but a short time before. Two of them must have been the pack animals, while the others included Nick Ribsam's Jack, and the three belonging to Bell Rickard and his two companions.

Their course along the eastern base of the hills showed the riders were searching for a favorable point of entrance. This looked as if the party was not fully familiar with the section, though it was by no means certain this was so.

Herbert began to feel misgivings, as he observed the twilight deepening into darkness, while the trail still kept the same course, varying a little now and then to the right or left with the changing course of the elevation.

By and by, the gloom became so pronounced that he drew his pony down to a walk, and, leaning over the saddle, studied the ground with the closest scrutiny. It was not long before this proved insufficient and he again dismounted.

"It makes slow work," he said, "but it is sure—well, I'll be hanged!"

Again there were no footprints before him! The ground showed not the least impression when he struck a match and stooped over.

"We can't be far off the track, Jill; we must now take the back trail, as the hunters say."

Holding the bridle in his left hand, he began carefully retracing his steps; but, instead of hunting for the path, he looked for the point where it had turned in among the hills. This must be close at hand, for the footprints were lost only a short time before.

He had advanced a little more than a hundred yards, when he observed an opening among the stunted vegetation and bowlders wide enough to allow a horse to pass through without trouble.

"This looks as if it might be the right place," he said, stopping and scrutinizing it; "we'll soon find out."

Another lucifer was called into play. He bent down, holding it before his head; and, as the tiny flame spread, he uttered an exclamation of delight. He had recovered the trail!

CHAPTER XIX.

IN THE RAVINE.

THE discovery that he was so near the party caused Herbert's heart to beat faster than usual. He felt the need of prudence and caution at every step, since he could not know whether Rickard was aware of his pursuit. It might be that the fellow had discovered it and laid an ambush for him.

But, in accordance with his previous resolution, he pushed on, leading his pony by the bridle, until he had penetrated a number of rods among the hills, when he once more paused.

He was struck by the resemblance between the ridge and the one where he had spent the previous night. The curious exception, however, was that the trail that he was following was without any ascent. Thus it was that, when he stopped, he found the rocks and trees rising on either hand, as if he was entering a cañon or deep ravine. The ground showed no grass, but was so gravelly under his feet, and so filled with stones and hollows, that he was sure a torrent or river, at some time or other, had forced its way over the bed.

That which checked him abruptly was his stepping into a pool of water, into which one foot sank to the knee. He hastily drew back, with a slight gasp caused by its coolness, and then, observing nothing distinctly in the gloom, struck a match.

The air was as still as in a vault, and it was unnecessary to shade the little blaze which he held in front and above his head.

The pool was so narrow that he could easily leap to the other side. It was clear, and Jill showed his appreciation of the boon by thrusting his nose into it and drinking his fill. Herbert himself was thirsty enough to lie down on his face and do the same.

He found that the ravine which he had entered had a varying width of a dozen to fifty feet, with precipitous sides, composed of such a mass of jagged and projecting rocks that it was easy to climb out of it from any point.

Not a particle of grass was visible, though possibly it was to be found further on.

Herbert's conclusion was that the ravine cut through the hills, and had been used by Rickard and his party to reach the other side. Whether he was correct or not remained to be learned.

It struck him, however, as imprudent to take his pony further. The sound of his hoofs were quite certain to betray him to anyone on the watch, while the youth himself could steal forward without noise. The light of the burning match had revealed a gnarled root projecting from the side of the ravine. He carefully tied the bridle to this, for the place was so unique in its way that he was resolved to take no chances of Jill going astray. He would lose nothing by the detention, because, as has been shown, food was unobtainable and his master did not expect to be long absent.

Pausing a minute to make sure his pony was securely fastened, Herbert pushed into the ravine, on the alert for the first sign of the criminals and their prisoner. It was an impressive situation, and, mindful of his slight mishap, he moved with great care, occasionally burning a match when afraid of a misstep.

Ten minutes after leaving his horse, he turned an abrupt bend in the ravine and was startled by observing the light of a camp fire. It was only a little way ahead, and directly in front, so that, had he continued his walk without variation, he must have stepped into the blaze itself.

The gorge, which was comparatively narrow up to this point, expanded into a width of fully a hundred yards, in the middle of which a large fire had been kindled, that lit up the surrounding gloom, and threw a faint illumination almost to the feet of Herbert, who stood silently studying it.

That the site was well chosen was proven by the gleam of another pool of water, much larger than the former, while a patch of green grass extended from the fire beyond until lost in the darkness.

The first glance at the camp was with the conviction that he had overtaken the party he was after, but the second look raised strong doubts in his mind, for he failed to observe that which until that moment he was confident of seeing.

The party that he had followed so far across the prairie, consisted of four horsemen, one of whom was Nick Ribsam, but only two were now in sight, and neither was the lad. Nor were the pack horses visible.

The reader must not forget that Herbert was asleep during Bell Rickard's forced visit to camp the night before and a long distance had separated the two until now. It was impossible, therefore, for him to know whether either of the parties before him was that worthy or not.

The light of the fire was sufficiently strong to bring out in relief the two horses, grazing on the luxuriant patch of grass, but, as I have said, no other animals were in sight.

One man was sitting on a stone near the fire, smoking a pipe, while the other stood in front of him, whittling a stick in the indifferent fashion that a person shows when his thoughts are otherwise occupied. He faced the one sitting on the bowlder, and the murmur of their voices was heard, as they talked, though no words were intelligible.

They were dressed in cowboy fashion, with their broad-brimmed hats, long hair, hickory shirts, and slouchy trousers tucked in their boot tops, not forgetting the belt around the waist for cartridges and pistols.

Herbert judged they were white men, though it was easy to be mistaken, since they might have been of mixed blood without its being betrayed in the firelight. He fancied one was the notorious horse thief, Belden Rickard, and the other the equally well-known half-breed, Jim-John; but this had to remain conjecture until someone confirmed or disproved it.

The bitter disappointment was his failure to see Nick, who he was confident of overtaking at the first camp reached. The only theory by which he could explain matters was that the party had divided, and one of the men had pushed on with Nick as his companion. If this were so, that one must have been Rickard. Possibly he feared pursuit, and was using the darkness to get further on with the pack horses, which could not travel as fast as the others. This might be readily done, a rendezvous having been agreed upon beforehand.

Herbert remained, viewing the fire, for a time, thinking it possible that Nick and the other man might put in an appearance, but as the minutes passed, he was confirmed in the belief named.

He determined to continue the hunt until he learned the truth. The expansion of the ravine where the fire had been kindled was so great that he could readily pass it without detection, but it would hardly do to venture upon so uncertain a journey on foot, when there was urgent need of a horse.

His plan, therefore, was to return for his pony and try to flank the camp, by leading him past. If he were discovered and challenged, he would boldly advance and make his business known, demanding that he be told where he could find his missing friend.

He took a parting look at the couple in whom he was so interested. They held the same positions as before, one sitting on the stone smoking, and the other standing in front, slowly whittling, while they discussed some matter in which neither seemed to feel a very deep interest.

Nothing was to be gained by waiting, and Herbert started back to get his horse. He had fixed the points so well in mind, that, when he supposed he was near the pool and ignited a match, he saw he was on the edge of it. He leaped lightly across, and, with the tiny flame still in his hand, walked to where his pony was tied a short time before.

Jill was gone! Since he could not have freed himself, someone had removed him.

While Herbert stood silent and dismayed, he caught the sound of a footfall, accompanied by a chuckle of triumph.

CHAPTER XX.

REINFORCEMENTS.

HERBERT WATROUS was dumfounded. He had stolen up the ravine and spent some time in studying the cam pfire and the two strangers, and now, on his return to where his pony had been tied, the animal was gone. While he was acting the spy, the same trick had been successfully played on him.

But he roused quickly, and running a few steps in the direction of the retreating horse and his captor, called:

"Stop, or I'll shoot! You can't steal my animal!"

It was an idle threat, for, in the gloom, he only knew the direction taken by the man and beast, and his shot, therefore, must have been at random.

"Shoot if you want to," was the defiant reply; "but the flash of your gun will give us the show to drop *you!*"

Surely he had heard *that* voice before.

"Strubell, is that you?" he called, still hurrying forward, but with his weapon lowered.

Two persons now laughed, and the well-known tones of the Texan called back:

"You'll have to practise a while, young man, before you learn how to trail Indians and horse thieves."

Delighted beyond measure, Herbert quickly joined the friends, whom he had hardly expected to meet again.

"I was afraid you were killed," said he, "and had no idea you were near me. Where did you come from?"

"We have been following you most of the day," said Strubell, "but your horse went so fast we couldn't overtake you, and, when you slowed him down, we concluded to let you go ahead, while we learned what you were driving at."

"When you are at this business," added Lattin, "you want to keep an eye to the rear as well as to the front."

The Texans had their own ponies with them,

and, so far as could be judged in the gloom, were suffering no ill effect from their sharp brush with their enemies the night before.

"Why did you take my horse?" asked Herbert.

"We wanted to give you a little scare, but you came back sooner than we expected. I followed after you, and, while you were viewing the camp fire, I did the same. I walked in front of you on the return, but your Jill was tied so fast that it took me longer than I expected to unfasten him."

"Did you see Belden at the camp up the ravine?"

"No; and you didn't either, for he isn't there."

"Who are those follows?"

"One is Jim-John the half breed, and the other a fellow named Brindage—Homer Brindage, I believe."

"They belong to Rickard's gang?"

"Yes—two worse scamps never went unhanged; I was afraid you were going forward to talk with them, and stood ready to stop you, if you made the start."

"Why, that's exactly what I would have done, if Nick had been with them," said the surprised Herbert; "would they have harmed me?"

"You would have found out mighty sudden; they are the kind that shoot first, and inquire afterward whether there was any reason for their haste."

While the brief conversation was going on, Strubell remounted his horse and the lad did the same. Lattin had been in the saddle from the first.

"You had a fight with them last night?"

"How did you know that?" asked Lattin

"I heard the sounds of your guns as well as theirs."

"I guess not," replied the Texan, "we didn't have any scrimmage with them."

"But there was plenty of firing."

"Nobody denies *that*, but I'm tellin' you the truth, when I say we haven't traded a single shot with Bell Rickard or any of his men."

Since the Texan had made this remark, Herbert expected he would follow it with an explanation of the previous night's experience. He did not deny that there had been a fight, only that Rickard and his men were not in it. With whom, therefore, were their shots exchanged?

Both Strubell and Lattin showed the same annoying reticence about certain matters that they had displayed more than once before. Neither offered a reply to the question that was asked by Herbert's expressive silence, which lasted for some moments.

A touch of impatience disturbed the youth. He felt like Nick when similarly annoyed. If they chose to affect so much mystery, he was not the one to gratify them by showing curiosity.

But a more important subject filled his mind. The fate of Nick Ribsam outweighed everything else, and on that he was not to be denied all the information they could furnish. Their help was needed and that without delay.

"From what you have said, Strubell, there is no doubt that Rickard has ridden away with Nick."

"I agree with you that far."

"Where has he gone?"

"How can you expect me to know any more about that than you?"

"But you *do* know more. What do you suppose?"

"They are pushing toward New Mexico."

"But that is hundreds of miles off."

"That doesn't hinder their riding that way more than it does us; they may never get there, but I suspect they are aiming for that country."

"Do you believe Rickard is an enemy of Nick?"

"There's no doubt of it; that little affair last night, which he must have explained to you, has stirred up all the ugliness in Bell's nature, and he is full of it."

"What do you think he means to do with Nick?"

"I would like to answer that question," said Strubell, who evidently sympathized with his young friend; "but I cannot."

"Do you fear he means to kill him?"

"I *hope* not."

"Heavens," exclaimed the agonized Herbert, "and are we to sit here and allow such a crime to be committed?"

"We are going to do our best to prevent it," was the response of Lattin, which struck fire in the hearts of the others.

"Yes," spoke Strubell again, "that's what we're here for; but before going further, I want you to tell me what took place after you left us yesterday afternoon."

"I can't tell you all, though most of it."

Thereupon, Herbert gave his experience with the norther, when for a while he believed he was doomed to freeze to death, ending with his search for Nick and the discovery, through the aid of his field glass, that he was riding away in company with Rickard and his companions. He had followed the party, doubting whether he could do anything to help him, but determined not to stay behind while Nick was in peril.

"Well," said Strubell, who, like Lattin, listened attentively to the story, "you must understand that we shall never let up till we have straightened out this matter. Rickard has started toward New Mexico, and he means to get there with the boy; the two are riding hard at this minute and will press their horses to the utmost."

"But what is their purpose?" asked the mystified Herbert.

"What is to be gained by puzzling our heads over the meaning of things, when we have the things themselves to deal with? I have my suspicion of what Bell is driving at, but I must get a little further along before I say what it is. Lattin disagrees with me, and a fellow doesn't like to find he's mistaken. Let that go while we bend all our energies toward righting the wrong."

"It strikes me as strange that if Rickard is in such haste, he should take the pack horses with him."

"He hasn't."

"But they are not in camp," said Herbert.

"No; he has taken them to some point not far off, probably on the other side of the hills, where they will be left for Brindage and Jim-John to take care of. You understand the object of this," the Texan hastened to add; "they want to give the impression that they are going slow, as they would have to do if they kept the pack animals with them. That is to throw dust in the eyes of Nick's friends; but you can depend upon it that it is not far from camp that they have left them, and they are now devoting themselves to speed. You know that pony of your friend is as fleet as any in this crowd."

"There is no doubt of that; Nick is a good judge of horses, and he studied him closely in San Antonio before buying him."

"Well, Bell has had so many dealings in the same line that you can make up your mind, when he trusts his worthless life on the back of an animal, that creature must know something about grabbing ground."

"That being so, tell me what your plan is, Strubell."

"Now it happens that Baker and I know a little more about this part of the country than Bell and his folks, though this isn't the first time they have traveled through it; they think this ravine is the only pass through the hills, for a long distance, but there's where they make a mistake."

"But what of that?"

"We'll take a ticket over the new route."

This odd remark caused a laugh from Lattin, who, unlike Herbert, caught its whole significance.

CHAPTER XXI.

THE PURSUIT.

MEN trained in the profession of the cowboys think and act quickly. Within a half hour following their meeting with Herbert Watrous, the party were travelling the other way, and shortly after emerged from the hills, where the ground was perfectly level, and advantage could be taken of the faint moonlight which would soon aid them.

As soon as they were fairly out in the open country, the Texans halted and sat motionless for a moment. They were listening for sounds which they heard not. Then Lattin slipped from the saddle and held his ear for a full minute pressed flat against the earth.

"It's all right," he remarked, swinging himself over the back of his pony. The three broke into a moderate gallop, riding almost abreast, for there was abundant room for them to do so.

It was about a mile from where the last change of direction took place that Strubell drew his horse down to a walk and edged in as close as he could to the hills, his companions, of course, doing the same. It was apparent that he was looking for the "new route" that had been spoken of. Herbert did all he could to aid, but when an abrupt change was made he saw no cause for it.

"That's the reason why so few know about this," explained the elder Texan, after stating that they had struck the right spot; "if it was plain enough to be seen miles off, Bell would have known all about it."

"Ard and me found it out by accident," added Lattin; "you obsarve how you turn here, just as if you was passing behind a door, before you hit the pass: that door hides it from the sight of anyone out on the prairie."

The peculiar conformation had been noticed by Herbert, who replied that he could not have noticed it at noonday.

"The queerest thing," added Lattin, "is that it's just the same on the other side ; if it wasn't, the pass would have been found from that direction; me and Ard was chasin' a couple of Kioways one day that had stolen a horse, when they dodged in here and gave us the slip; that's the way we hit it."

An expert engineer could not have constructed a finer cut through the ridge—that is, for the present purpose. At no place was it more than a hundred or less than fifty feet in width, and the ground was so level that, had they chosen, their horses might have galloped the whole distance. There was little doubt that the ridge had been broken apart at this point by some terrific convulsion of nature, the opposite sides corresponding so perfectly that they would have dovetailed, could they have been pushed together.

This being the fact, a brief time only elapsed, when the three horsemen, whose sole purpose now was to overtake the party that was making off with Nick Ribsam, rode out upon the open plain beyond.

Here was another brief halt, while the younger Texan held his ear against the earth, the other neither moving nor speaking. He remained in his prone posture so long that it was evident he had detected something. He must have caught a suspicious sound and was trying to locate it.

"It's right ahead," he said, as he once more climbed into the saddle, "and not fur off."

Since the movements were now based on the discovery of the younger cowboy, the elder dropped slightly back and joined Herbert as an intimation that Lattin had become the leader.

The latter kept his pony on a walk, and the youth was close enough to him to observe that he frequently turned his head in different directions, showing that he was looking and listening with the utmost care. All at once he drew rein and the others halted by his side.

"*Sh!* you hear 'em," he whispered.

Herbert noticed the stamp of a horse, as he judged it to be, which could not have been far in advance, though the night was so still that a slight sound could be heard a long way. He was tempted to ask whether it was not true that if they could discover others close by, the strangers had the same chance of learning about them, but he was sure his friends understood themselves too well to commit a blunder which *he* would detect.

Without another word between the men the younger let himself silently to the ground and moved forward in the gloom. It seemed to the youth that he showed rashness by this act, for, instead of crouching over and stealing along, step by step, he remained erect and walked with his ordinary gait, except perhaps he lifted and set down his feet more lightly.

It need not be said, however, that Baker Lattin understood what he was doing, and, when at the end of a few minutes he came back, he brought the very news which Strubell expected and which confirmed the theory formed by the cowboys.

The three pack horses belonging to the Americans were less than two hundred yards distant. A couple were lying down while the third was cropping the grass. No person was nearer than the owners, so that it was proven that they had been left there by Bell Rickard and his companion to be picked up by Jim-

John and Brindage, who were to follow them at a more leisurely pace.

The animals were not picketed, for they were not likely to wander beyond easy reach during the few hours that must elapse before the rear guard could come up with them. Their loads had been placed on the ground and their bridles removed, so that they were free to wander whither they chose.

The tidings were pleasing to our friends, who were thus given the means of procuring what they were sure to need before reaching the end of their journey. Strubell brought forth the blankets, extra suits for stormy weather, and a goodly number of articles that insured comfort for a good while to come.

It seemed odd that after recovering their animals and property the Texans should coolly turn them over to the thieves, but the reader will see that it was the only thing to be done. Rickard and Slidham had abandoned them for the sake of speed, and for their pursuers to take them up would be to handicap themselves in the same fatal fashion.

The fugitives, as they may be called, had

got what they wanted from the pack horses, and, when Strubell and Lattin did the same, the loads were much lightened.

It was, therefore, without the slightest hesitation that, after procuring their supplies, our friends resumed their advance, leaving the couple among the hills to explain by what means the Texans had flanked them.

Strubell had hopes of overtaking Rickard and Slidham before daylight, his belief being that they would go into camp after riding a number of miles. They had been in the saddle so continuously during the last few days, it would seem they ought to need rest as much as their animals, but as the darkness wore on without sight or sound of them, he and Lattin agreed that the scamps were pushing their horses to the utmost.

The pursuers were also pressing their animals hard, and to a higher degree than they would have done under other circumstances, but the Texans showed an eagerness to reach the other party that caused Herbert alarm. He was certain there must be a cause for this haste which they refused to explain to him.

At long intervals one of the men resorted to the usual test of placing his ear to the ground with the hope of catching the sounds of footsteps. Once he stated that he heard something of the kind, and for a half hour they believed they were coming up with the company in front. It proved, however, that some kind of animals were moving across the country that were not likely to be those they were seeking.

To settle the question the pursuit was forced, and they overtook a couple of mavericks or stray cattle. One of them was turned to account, for Strubell shot it, and the party went into camp.

It was high time they did so, for their ponies were worn out and they themselves were tired and sleepy. Enough fuel was found to start a fire, over which a good meal was prepared, sufficient being cooked and laid aside to allow them to keep up the pursuit for a couple of days without stopping for food.

The fear of Herbert Watrous was that a mistake had been made by his friends who had wandered from the trail, but when daylight dawned, and the Texans made an investigation, they found they were right. Rickard and Slidham were following the very course named by them—that is, in the direction of New Mexico.

"It looks as if it's going to be a long chase," said Strubell; "but unless something unexpected happens we shall win."

CHAPTER XXII.

ACROSS THE BORDER.

NOW came several days' experience, so similar in its main features that it is not worth while to describe it in detail.

The Texans and Herbert Watrous pushed their ponies to the verge of prudence; but though the skill of the cowboys saved them from going astray, and there never was any danger of losing the trail of the fugitives, they failed to catch sight of them during that period.

They knew that Nick Ribsam rode a horse fully the equal, if not the superior, of those following him, and it was shown that Bell Rickard and Harman Slidham were well mounted. It was easy, therefore, for the three to cover the same ground as their pursuers, and, having as good a start, there was little prospect of the parties gaining sight of each other until those in advance chose to permit it.

Herbert Watrous will never forget that long ride through Western Texas. Had he not undergone a severe preparation he never could have stood it, for it seemed to him that he was in the saddle all the time, except when stretched on the earth asleep. Jill, his faithful pony, developed astonishing endurance, but though the Texans got everything possible out of the animals, they were too prudent to force them to a killing pace; all stood it well.

During that extended ride many streams were crossed. One of them was the North Fork of the Concho, properly the Colorado, on which the capital of Texas stands. Although at certain seasons this becomes a raging torrent, the horses forded it from bank to bank without once losing their feet. Indeed, only for a few paces did the water touch the stirrups of the riders.

There were other banks, separated by hundreds of feet, down which they rode into deep beds, where the signs showed the streams ran full at certain times with an enormous volume of water, but, like the current of the upper

Rio Grande, they seemed dried up. Here and there were muddy pools, connected by tiny threads of water, which hardly moved, while elevations of the beds were met midway between the shores, where the hoofs of their horses actually stirred the dust.

In some portions of Texas the rise and subsidence of the streams are as sudden as those of Central Australia. At none of the numerous crossings were our friends obliged to swim their animals.

On the third day they were checked by a norther, which caught them in the middle of the plain, where nothing in the nature of a shelter was available. But the Texans met the crisis in an odd way.

First blanketing their ponies, they scooped out small, circular holes in the ground, into which they placed dried buffalo chips, and dried blades of grass. When these were fairly burning they folded their blankets about their bodies so as to envelop their heads, and then sat over the openings, allowing enough space to save the fires from being smothered. While the situation had its discomforts, it afforded a grateful degree of warmth, which none enjoyed more than Herbert, who could not help laughing at the comical figures they made.

The norther, which fortunately did not last long, was followed by a cold, drizzling rain, which would have been uncomfortable to the last degree but for the slickers of oiled linen that had been provided for such emergencies. The Texans, when they overtook the pack animals, made certain that these garments were secured, for it was inevitable that the long ride before them should be marked by occasional bad weather.

It was impossible to obtain good camping grounds at all times, though the party did not often suffer in this respect. While now and then they went a day with only a single meal, it cannot be said they actually suffered; but the main purpose of the pursuers was speed, and they were exasperated to find how cleverly Rickard held his own. Not only that, but there was reason to fear he was drawing away from them. It was impossible, even with the wonderful woodcraft of the pursuers, to make sure of this, for several hours cannot show a perceptible difference in the trail of three horsemen; but the Texans insisted that there was greater space between them than at the hour of opening the pursuit.

Since it was not believed that Rickard had a field glass with him, the pursuers would have gained a great advantage could they have got nigh enough to see him, which was the very thing they were unable to do.

I must not forget to make known one important fact. You will remember the real cause of Herbert Watrons' journey across Texas, which was to regain the health that was seriously threatened by his bad habits and rapid growth. While he received vast benefit from breathing the pure air of the South-west, it was his forced march, as it may be called, to New Mexico that did the splendid work for him.

The continuous exercise, the crystalline atmosphere, the deep, refreshing sleep, the abstention from tobacco, nourishing food (which, though only partially cooked and eaten at long intervals, was the very best diet he could have obtained), in short the "roughing it," in the truest sense, was the true "elixir of life," and wrought a change in the young man which, could his parents have witnessed, they would have pronounced marvellous.

The sickly complexion was succeeded by a ruddy brown, the effect of the wind, storms, and sun; his shoulders straightened, his slight, hacking cough vanished, and he felt every morning, noon, and night that he was gaining strength and health.

It has been said that no perfectly healthy person can suffer depression of spirits for a long time. Nature will rebound and lift him above the gloom. Herbert Watrous wondered more than once, while riding across the prairie, or lying upon the grass, or springing into the saddle in the morning, that he should be so buoyant and hopeful when the youth whom he loved best in all the world was in peril of his life. He reproved himself that he should feel thus, but, all the same, he could not help it.

This lightness of spirits was not wholly due

to his rapidly improving health, but to the fact that he was convinced there was a growing reason to hope for the best. Whatever the vicious Rickard might intend to do with Nick Ribsam in the way of revenge, it was clear his instant taking off did not form a part of the scheme. The fact that, as the day passed, Nick still kept his place among the living, was good ground for hoping that he would continue to do so indefinitely. Better still, Strubell and Lattin agreed with him, though neither was as sanguine as Herbert himself.

There came one of those bright, perfect days, when the sunshine seemed more golden, the air clearer, and the sky bluer than is ever seen elsewhere. Herbert noticed that his companions were unusually interested in the surrounding scenery. The prairie was mostly of the rolling kind, though not to a marked degree, and the grass was so plentiful and succulent that the grazing could not have been improved. They had forded a small stream, and, gazing in any direction, nothing but the same apparently endless plain greeted the eye.

Not a hill or mountain range was perceived in any portion of the horizon.

"Herbert," said Strubell, looking across from his saddle, "in what part of the world do you suppose we are?"

"Why," replied the youth, surprised by the question, "we must be well advanced into Western Texas."

"We are in New Mexico," said the Texan, with a smile, "and have been there for twenty-four hours."

"That's good news, though I was expecting it before long."

"I wasn't sure of the exact spot where we crossed the border, but it took place yesterday; we are beyond the twenty-sixth meridian, with the Sand Hills far to the east of us, and north of the thirty-second parallel."

"And how much further to the ranch?"

"The Pecos is less than fifty miles away, and just on the other side of that is Mr. Lord's ranch. Hello!" he added, quickly bringing his glass to his eyes; "we have seen a few Indians, but, if I am not mistaken, yonder comes a white man."

Herbert was quick to bring his glass into use, and instantly saw that his friend was right. An individual was drawing near who was destined to play an important part in the stirring incidents at hand.

CHAPTER XXIII.

A RELIC OF OTHER DAYS.

I MUST not omit to say that during the days occupied in the long ride toward the northwest, our friends saw Indians more than once. They were generally straggling parties, who viewed the three horsemen with as much curiosity as our friends studied them. They were either Comanches or Kioways, though the hunting grounds of the latter were far to the eastward. Close to the New Mexican boundary they observed a half dozen warriors, who the Texans said were Apaches. They followed the whites for one afternoon, discharging their guns from a distance, and more than once seemed on the point of attacking them; but a shot from Lattin wounded a dusky raider badly, after which all drew off and were seen no more.

The sight of a white man riding toward them, with the evident purpose of a meeting, centred the interest of the three on him. He was mounted on a wiry "plug," and as he drew near was seen to be one of those individuals occasionally met in the wildest parts of the great West a generation ago. He belonged to the trappers and hunters, who, leaving the confines of civilization at the close of the summer season, spent the severe winters in trapping beavers, otters, and other fur-bearing animals. They faced the perils of vengeful red men, wild beasts, and the rigorous winters for the sake of the pittance paid at the frontier posts and towns for the scant peltries carried thither.

The man who rode up had but the single animal, his worldly possessions being strapped in place behind him, while his long, old-fashioned rifle rested across the saddle in front. His dress may be described as a cross between that of a cowboy and an Indian. His hat was of the sombrero order, but he wore a skin hunting shirt, leggings and moccasins, and possessed a massive frame which must have been the repository of immense strength.

His face was a study. His hair was long,

and, like the beard that covered his face, plentifully sprinkled with gray. His small eyes were light in color, restless, bright, and twinkling; his nose large and Roman in form, and his voice a mellow bass.

The trapper was yet several rods distant when Lattin exclaimed in a surprised undertone:

"Why, that's old Eph, as sure as I live!"

"So it is," added Strubell; "I haven't seen him for years."

The hunter recognized the Texan at the same moment, and the movement of his heavy beard showed he was smiling, though it was impossible to see his mouth. He uttered a hearty salutation as he came forward, and grasped each hand in turn, being introduced by Strubell to Herbert, who noticed the searching look he fixed for a moment on his face.

"I'm glad to know you, younker," he said, almost crushing his hand; "but I'm s'prised to meet you so soon after seeing another; I aint used to running agin boys in this part of the world; but things seem to be gettin' endways the last few years, and I've made up my mind thar's powerful little in the trappin' bus'ness any longer."

Eph Bozeman, as Strubell announced him, proved by the words just uttered that he had seen Nick Ribsam, and therefore must have news to impart. Since he had come directly over the trail of the horse thieves, the Texans had suspected the other fact before he made it known.

After the exchange of a few questions and answers, during which Bozeman stated that he was on his way to Austin to hunt up an old friend, who had been engaged for a number of years in buying and selling mustangs, Strubell explained the business that had brought him and his companions over the border into New Mexico.

"How far are we behind Rickard and the others?"

The trapper turned in his saddle and looked to the rear for a few seconds without speaking. His forehead was wrinkled with thought, but it did not take him long to answer the question.

"You are thirty-five miles or tharabouts

from the Pecos, and Bell and Harman will cross the stream about noon, which is two hours off, so you may say thar is thirty miles atween you."

"There wasn't more than a dozen when we started," was the remark of the disgusted Lattin, "so we have been losing ground for more than a week that we've been chasing 'em."

"Thar can't be any doubt of that 'cordin' to your own words," replied the trapper; "but if you keep on you'll be up with 'em by the end of two days."

"How do you make that out?" asked Strubell.

"'Cause they're goin' to stop at the ranch layin' just beyond."

Strubell and Lattin exchanged glances, and Herbert, who was watching them, was satisfied that the news did not surprise them. They had expected it from the first or they would not have persevered thus far.

"I met 'em yesterday," continued Bozeman, "not fur back; they had halted to cook a young antelope that Harman shot, and I jined in on the chorus."

"What did they say to you?"

"Nothin' in partic'lar; I told 'em whar I was goin', and asked 'em what they war doin' in this part of the world. They said they war on thar way to look at that ranch I spoke about on t'other side of the Pecos, and it might be they would spend some time thar."

"Did they say anything about the boy with them?" asked Herbert, whose curiosity was at the highest point.

"Yas—consid'rable. I asked who he was and whar he come from; Bell told me he was a younker as wanted to take a trip through Texas fur his health—though he's the healthiest younker I've looked on for many a day—and tharfur they war takin' him along."

"Did you have anything to say to Nick?"

"Who's Nick?" asked the trapper, with another movement of the beard around his mouth that showed he was smiling.

"He's the boy—my friend that we're looking after."

"I shook hands with him, give him some

good advice that he thanked me for, and that was all."

"I suppose he was afraid to say anything more."

"It must have been that; Bell and Harman watched him powerful close, and though he looked as if he would like to add something, he didn't. I tell you," continued the trapper, addressing Strubell and the others, "I s'pected something was wrong, though I didn't say nothin', 'cause thar warn't any show for me doin' anything. I'm s'prised to hear what you say, and, boys, if you want me to give you any help, I'm yours to command."

This was said with a heartiness that left no doubt of its sincerity. His friends were delighted with the offer, and Herbert especially was sure that no better thing could happen. He assured old Eph he should be well paid for his trouble. The trapper did not refuse, though his proposal was made without any idea of the kind; but, as he confessed, matters had gone ill with him for a long time, and he was in need of all he could honestly earn.

He had known Rickard and Slidham for ten

years, and was aware of the crooked business in which they were engaged; but, inasmuch as they did not cross his path, there was no cause to quarrel with them. He had spent more than one night in their company, and would not hesitate to do so again, without misgiving; but when he learned of their highhanded outrage, his sturdy nature was filled with wrath, and he declared himself eager not only to help rescue the boy, but to punish them for their crime.

This decision was reached within ten minutes after the handshaking, and the trapper wheeled his pony around and joined in the pursuit without further delay.

Since it was clear that the others could not be overtaken until they made their final halt, the pursuers let down in their pace, and allowed their animals to follow at a leisurely rate.

It struck Herbert as very strange that the destination of the enemies and friends of Nick Ribsam should be the same. Though the former could not have caught sight of their pursuers, they must have known of it, and were now about to stop and give them time to come up, and make battle, if they chose, for the possession of the young man, who, without any fault of his own, had become the bone of contention.

There was something about the business that he could not understand; but by listening to the stealthy conversation of his friends he gained an inkling of the truth. He learned, too, that they were less hopeful of success than he. The almost endless pursuit, however, was drawing to a close, and the end, whatever it might be, was at hand.

CHAPTER XXIV.

A RACE WITH AN AVALANCHE.

THE little party had encamped in a hollow in the prairie, where, after eating their sparse lunch, they lolled on the ground, the men smoking their pipes, while their animals cropped the grass before lying down for the rest which they needed as much as their owners.

"Yes," said Eph Bozeman, after the conversation had lasted a half hour, and took the form of reminiscences on the part of the adults, "I war eighteen years old when I went on my first trappin' hunt with my old friend Kit Carson, and there war three trappers beside us. I war younger in them days than now, and I don't quite understand how Kit come to let me do one of the foolishest things a younker of my age ever tried.

"It war in the fall of the year that we five went away up in the Wild River Mountain, meanin' to stay thar till spring. Kit had been in the same region a few years before, but he said no trap had ever been set in the place, and we was sure of makin' a good haul before the winter war over. It was November, and we went to work at once. We were purty well north, and so high up that I don't think warm weather ever strikes the place.

"We had good luck from the start, and by the time snow began to fly had stowed away in the cave we fixed up for our winter quarters more peltries than Kit had took the whole season before. That was good; but when we begun to figure up how much money we war going to have to divide down at Bent's Fort, after the winter war over, from the sale of the furs, Kit shook his head and said the season warn't ended yet.

"Since we war sure of having ugly weather we had got ready for it. The luggage that war strapped to the back of our pack mules had a pair of snow-shoes for each of us, and we all knowed how to use 'em.

"The first snow-fall come in the beginnin' of December, but it didn't amount to much.

Howsumever, we catched it the next week, heavy. It begun comin' down one afternoon just as it war growin' dark. It war thin and sand-like, and when it hit our faces stung like needle p'ints. Carson went outside, and after studyin' the sky as best he could, when he couldn't see it at all, said it war goin' to be the storm of the winter.

"He war right, as he generally war in such matters. When mornin' come it war snowin' harder than ever, and it never let up for four days and nights. Then when it stopped the fall war mor'n a dozen feet in the mountains. This settled like, and a crust formed on top, which war just the thing for our snow-shoes. On the steep inclines you've only to brace yourself and let the law of gravertation, as I b'lieve they call it, do the rest.

"It war powerful lonely in our cave day after day, with nothing to do but to talk and smoke and sleep, and now and then steal out to see if the mules war safely housed. It got so bad after a while that we all put on our snow-shoes and started out for a little fun.

"About a mile off we struck a gulch which

we had all seen many times. It war the steepest that we knowed of within fifty miles. From the top to whar it broadened out into a valley war three-quarters of a mile, and all the way war like the roof of a house. I s'pose it war a little more than a hundred yards wide at the top, whar the upper part of the biggest kind of an avalanche had formed. There the wind and odd shape of the rocks and ground had filled the place with snow that war deeper than the tallest meetin'-house you ever laid eyes on. It had drifted and piled, reachin' far back till it war a snow mountain of itself. Don't you forget, too," added the trapper impressively, "that this snow warn't loose drift stuff, but a solid mass that, when it once started, would go down that gulch like so much rock, if you can think of a rock as big as that.

"We war standin' and lookin' at this mountain of snow, wonderin' how long it would be before it would swing loose and plunge into the valley below, when a fool feelin' come over me. I turned to Kit and the other fellers and offered to bet a beaver skin that I could start even with the avalanche and beat it down into the valley. Carson wouldn't take the bet, for he saw what rashness it war. Yet he didn't try to dissuade me, and the other chaps took me up right off. The idea got into my head that Carson thought I war afraid, and then nothin' could have held me back.

"It didn't take us long to get things ready. One of the trappers went with me to see that the start war all right, while Kit and the other picked thar way to the valley below, so as to have a sight of the home stretch.

"It took us a good while, and we had to work hard to make our way to the foot of the avalanche. When we got thar at last and I looked up at that mountain of snow ready to tumble right over onto me, I don't mind sayin' I did feel weak in the knees; but I wouldn't have backed out if I knowed thar war only one chance in a million of my ever livin' to tell it.

"The chap with me said if I wanted to give it up it would be all right—he told me afterward that he war sorry he had took my bet—but I laughed, and told him it war a go.

"He helped me fix my snow-shoes, and wouldn't let me start till he seen everything war right. Then I stood on the edge of the gulch and held myself still by graspin' the corner of the rock behind me. He climbed above, so he could peep over and see me. He said I war so far below that I looked like a fly, and I know that he didn't look much bigger than that to me. It took him so long to climb to the perch that my hand was beginnin' to grow numb, when I heard his voice, faint and distant-like:

"'Hello, Eph, down thar! Are you ready?'

"'Yes, and tired of waitin',' I answered.

"'*One—two—three!*'

"As he said the last word, and it was so faint that I could hardly hear him, him and me fired our pistols at the same time, as you sometimes see at a foot race, though thar they ginerally have but the one pistol.

"You understand how it was," added the trapper for the benefit of Herbert Watrous: "them shots war fur the avalanche. Bein' as we war startin' on a foot race, it war right that we should have a fair start, and the only way of doin' that was by settin' off some gunpowder. If the avalanche was hangin', as it seemed to be, the shakin' of the air made by our pistols would set it loose and start it down the valley after me. But onless it war balanced just that way the broadside of a frigate wouldn't budge it.

"Howsumever, that war the lookout of the avalanche and not mine, but, bein' as I meant it should be fair and square, I waited after firin' my pistol, lookin' and listenin'. I didn't mean to start in ahead of the thing, nor did I mean it should get the best of me. As like as not it wouldn't budge, and then of course the race war off.

"For a second or two I couldn't hear nothin' but the moanin' of the wind away up where the other feller had climbed. Then I heard a sound like the risin' of a big storm. It war low and faint at first, but it quickly growed into the most awful roar mortal man ever heard. Just then my friend shouted:

"'*Here she comes! Off with you!*'

"I give myself a shove out over the top

of the snow, curvin' about, so that when I reached the middle of the gulch I started downward. In that second or two I seen the whole avalanche under way, hardly a hundred yards off, and it war comin' for me like a railroad train, and goin' faster every second.

"You can make up your mind that I war doin' some tall travellin' myself.

"Whew! boys, I can't tell you much about that race. The avalanche didn't flatten out and shoot down the gorge in loose masses, as I've seen 'em do, but just stuck together and come like one solid half of the mountain itself.

"If it catched me I was a goner just as sure as if run down by a steam-engine. But you would think thar couldn't be any chance of it catchin' me,' cause it war gravertation that was pullin' us both, and one oughter go as fast as t'other. The only thing I had to do was to keep my feet and stay in the middle of the gorge. If I catched one of my toes in the snow crust I would tumble, and before I could help myself the avalanche would squelch me.

"I can never forget, but I can't tell how I felt goin' down that three-quarters of a mile like a cannon ball. The wind cut my face as if it war a harrycane, and everything was so misty like I couldn't see anything plain, and so I war in mortal fear of turnin' out of the course and hittin' the side of the gulch.

"I don't know how it war, but once I felt myself goin' over. I s'pose I must have got out of line and tried to get back without exactly knowin' what I war doin'. Kit Carson, who war watchin' me, said I went two hundred feet balanced on one snow-shoe. He then give me up, for he war sure thar warn't a shadder of a chance for me.

"But I swung back agin, and, keepin' to the middle of the gulch, soon struck the level, and went skimmin' away as fast as ever till I begun goin' up the incline on t'other side. I war doin' that in fine style when the p'int of one of my shoes dipped under the snow crust, and I know I turned a round dozen summersets before I stopped. It sort of mixed things in my brain, but the snow saved me from gettin' hurt, and though the avalanche come powerful close, it didn't quite reach me, and I won my beaver skin."

CHAPTER XXV.

THE RANCH.

EPH BOZEMAN was so familiar with the Pecos River, from its source in the Rocky Mountains to its junction with the Rio Grande, that he conducted his friends to a fording place, where it was crossed without any of them wetting their feet. Riding up the opposite bank, they started across the comparatively level country, and by the middle of the afternoon struck a piece of grazing ground, which the hunters told him belonged to the ranch that the banker, Mr. Lord, had sent Strubell and Lattin to inspect.

The lands were so extensive that there were many portions from which not the first glimpse could be gained of the adobe structure that was erected nearly a half century before.

The little party pushed onward, and before the sun dipped below the horizon began the ascent of a moderate slope, from the top of which the coveted view could be obtained.

Since Rickard and his companion must have known of the pursuit, they would be on the lookout for the Texans, who were eager to befriend Nick Ribsam. It was decided not to allow them to know the cowboys had arrived in the vicinity before the following day. Strubell hinted that important events might be brought about between the setting and the rising of the sun.

Herbert, who began to feel a natural nervousness as the crisis approached, made several inquiries about Jim-John, the half-breed, and his companion, who had been left behind. Were they not likely to abandon the pack horses on discovering they had been flanked by the Texans, and hasten to the help of the couple that had been the first to cross over from Western Texas to New Mexico? But when Eph Bozeman agreed with Strubell and Lattin that there was nothing to be feared of that nature, Herbert bade good-by to his fears and fixed his attention on that which was in front.

Leaving their animals in the hollow, where they were safe against disturbance, the four climbed the elevation, the youth carrying one field glass, while Strubell had the other. The trapper had never used anything of the kind, and refused to do so now. He claimed that his eyes were as good as ever—and he was undoubtedly right—and he needed no artificial aid.

It looked like useless precaution, but on reaching the crest the party crouched low in order to render themselves less conspicuous.

"Thar she is!" said old Eph, extending his left hand to westward, while his right grasped his inseparable rifle; "and I'll bet them new-fangled machines won't show you anything more than I see this very minute."

A mile away stood a broad, firm building, of a slatish yellow color as seen through the clear air. It was of adobe or sun-dried bricks, which, in the course of time, had become compact and hard enough to resist a bombardment of six-pounders better than many forts erected for that purpose.

The land immediately surrounding the

"A mile away stood a broad, firm building."
Page 224.

structure was smooth and quite level, and covered with grass which wore a soft, beautiful tint, mellowed by the intervening distance. On the further side of the building were a few bushes, bearing a resemblance to the well known mesquite growth so common in many portions of the Southwest.

These were the main features of the scene when viewed by the unaided eye, but the helpful field glass added something.

Lying on his face, with his instrument pointed at the building, Herbert Watrous studied it closely. He offered the instrument to Lattin, but he, seeing how much the youth was interested, declined, and waited until Strubell was ready to pass the other to him.

The youth noted the broad door in the middle, with a small narrow window on either side of the upper story. The front was like that of an immense box, there being little slope to the roof. It was probably one of those mission houses built in the preceding century by the Jesuits, who devoted their lives to the conversion of the Indians, and that, having been abandoned by them as civilization advanced, had been taken possession of by those who secured a claim to the extensive tract which surrounded it.

Being questioned on this point, Bozeman as well as the Texans replied that such was undoubtedly the fact, for it was far different from the flimsy structures of wood used by ranchmen in other sections. There was a court inside, after the fashion of the older houses in Spanish countries, the building itself enclosing this open space, so that when manned by only a few, it was capable of withstanding the attack of a large force.

Bozeman stated further that the ranch was abandoned because of the Indians. While the men who made their homes there were safe so long as they stayed behind the wall, they could not afford to remain there. Hundreds of cattle had been killed or run off by the Apaches, whose chief hunting grounds are further west, until the ranchmen who essayed the business became discouraged and gave it up.

As a consequence, the place had been

allowed to run to waste for years. During that time the grazing had improved, though a large part of the thousands of acres had paid tribute to other cattlemen. Besides this, the marauding Apaches, with which our government was having much trouble at that time, were mainly in the western part of the territory and in Arizona. This made the ranch so inviting that it was beginning to attract attention, and when Mr. Lord, in San Antonio, was offered it for what was really a small sum, he was warranted in sending a couple of trustworthy experts to examine and report upon it.

This was the destination toward which the Texans and Herbert Watrous had been riding through many long days, and that was now in sight. By a strange order of things, which at present he could not understand, the ranch was the objective point also of the two evil men who held Nick Ribsam as prisoner.

He had puzzled his brain many times to read the meaning of all this; but though he had formed his theory, he forced himself to be content to wait until the Texans or events themselves should reveal the truth.

The most careful scrutiny of the front and eastern side of the adobe building failed to show any sign of life. That, however, was no proof that it was not there. The horsemen might have ridden abreast through the broad door, closing it after them, placed their horses within the numerous quarters facing the court within, and then, climbing to the roof, watch the eastern horizon for a sign of their pursuers.

Fully ten minutes passed without a word being spoken by our friends, who were inspecting the building from the crest of the elevation. They were so intent on their work that nothing else was thought of.

Having studied every foot that was visible, Herbert went over it again several times, but with no better success than at first. He was gifted with fine eye-sight, and, when he finally lowered his glass with a sigh, he glanced across at Strubell, who, having passed the other instrument to Lattin, was looking expectantly into the face of the youth.

"How did you make out?" he asked.

"I couldn't find anything at all," replied Herbert. "Did you?"

"Well, yes; Kickard, Slidham, and Nick are there, but a bigger surprise awaits *them* than *us*."

"What do you mean?"

"Point your glass over to the left," replied the Texan, "and I think you will see something that will surprise you."

CHAPTER XXVI

BELL RICKARD'S SCHEME.

HERBERT WATROUS turned his field glass to the left, and, for the first time since he caught sight of the adobe structure, gave attention to another part of his field of vision.

The cause of the Texan's remark was apparent. A half mile beyond the building was a party of horsemen, numbering perhaps a dozen. They were grouped together and apparently holding a discussion over some matter in which all must have been interested, since they kept in such close order.

The youth had become accustomed to seeing Indians since leaving San Antonio, and needed no one to tell him that these people belonged to that race. The distance was too far for them to show distinctly through the instrument, but enough was seen to settle the point.

"What tribe are they?" he asked, addressing all his companions. Strubell was studying them without the glass, while Lattin had turned his gaze thither, and Eph was lying on his face, his brows wrinkled, his gaze concentrated on the group. It was he who answered:

"'Paches, every one of them."

"Are they not off their hunting grounds?" asked Herbert.

"Not 'cordin' to thar ideas, for every 'Pache believes that the whole North American continent belongs to his people, which is about what every redskin thinks. Howsumever, they ginerally do thar killin' and deviltry further over in Arizona, but them's 'Paches sure as you're born."

"They seem to be as much interested in the building as we are."

"They've seen Rickard and Slidham and the younker go in thar, and they're tryin' to figure out what it means. You see things are in a quar' shape in these parts."

While the party lay on the crest of the elevation, looking at the building and the council of warriors beyond, Strubell for the first time showed a desire to make known to Herbert Watrous the things that had puzzled him. The strange enterprise had now reached a point where he was willing to talk. He had consulted with Lattin and Eph until there was an agreement all round, and no cause for further secrecy existed. In fact, there had never been any real cause for it at all.

Without quoting the Texan's words, it may be said that in the minds of the party it was clear that Belden Rickard, the noted horse thief, with his companion Harman Slidham, was carrying out a scheme to secure a ransom for the restoration of Nick Ribsam to his friends.

It will be remembered that Herbert had held this belief more than once, but he saw so many difficulties in the way that he was awaiting another explanation. He now asked Strubell to clear up the points that perplexed him, and he did, so far as he could.

He wished to learn why, if Rickard had formed the plan for the capture of Nick, with the idea of restoring him to freedom on the payment of a sum of money, he had ridden hundreds of miles to reach the point of conference, when it might as well have been held in Texas, and within sight of the very ridge where Nick fell into the power of his enemies. It was this phase of the question that had troubled Herbert greatly and led him to fear the ruffian intended to take the life of his friend.

Strubell replied that during the conversation with Rickard, whom he had known for years, he picked up more than one item of news which surprised him. One was that while making his long rides through the South-west, he and his companions, when hard pressed, were accustomed, at times, to take refuge in the old mansion house on the ranch which Mr. Lord proposed buying. This had been abandoned, as I have already stated, for years; but in the hospitable West, where every person's doors are open, no one would have hesitated to enter the adobe structure, whenever cause existed for doing so.

Rickard saw signs of others having been there, though he did not believe the Indians ever passed through the broad doors into the courtyard beyond. Had there been a party of settlers or white men within they would have been eager to do so, but while it was empty the incitement was lacking.

Rickard and his gang were in a peculiar situation. The Texans had reason to believe that he had fully twenty desperate associates in pushing his unlawful business over an immense extent of territory, though it was rare that they all came together. They were not only in danger from Indians, as were all who ventured into that section, but they were outlawed by their own race. It was dangerous for any member of the gang to trust himself within reach of the law, while the rough bordermen would have strung up every one without hesitation could they have laid hands on them.

Leading this wild, lawless life, it was necessary for these ruffians to have retreats, where they could feel comparatively safe. A number of such were at command. Some were deep in the mountains, and one was the abandoned ranch. Standing in the middle of a vast and comparatively level plain this had many advantages over the others, while it was also deficient in more than one respect.

Among the secret compartments in the old mission house was a store-room for provisions, where Rickard saw that enough grain was kept to last him and several companions for weeks. There was a spring of water that could not be shut off, so that a small garrison could stand an indefinite siege from a large number. In this place, the great horse thief and his followers, whether few or many, might feel safe.

Had Rickard, after securing the custody of Nick Ribsam, proposed his plan of ransom, he would have been in an awkward situation. Any messenger that he might send forward could be made prisoner by the Texans and held as a hostage. The little party itself was liable to be assailed and destroyed, for no mercy would have been showed at such a time, though a certain rude chivalry prevailed in other respects.

In what way would the situation be improved if Rickard took his prisoner to the adobe building? This was the question which

Herbert asked and the answer to which was simple.

Behind the walls of the massive structure it was easy for Rickard to communicate by word of mouth without any risk to himself. He need not send out a messenger to be captured, but could make known his terms to Nick's friends, who would be at liberty to accept or reject them.

It was the strong suspicion that such was the purpose of the ruffians that led the Texans to make every effort to overtake them before they reached their refuge. Could they have brought Rickard and his companion to bay they would have forced their own terms upon him.

But the criminal was too cunning thus to be caught. Leaving the pack horses for Jim-John and Brindage to look after, he pushed on with such vigor that, as we have shown, the refuge was attained in spite of all the pursuers could do to prevent it.

Rickard was an honest fellow in his early days and had done scouting duty in the company of Arden Strubell. It was this fact that

BELL RICKARD'S SCHEME. 237

led the latter to show him a certain consideration when he was made prisoner by Nick Ribsam, though there might have been other situations in which they would have flown at each other with irrestrainable wrath.

It was Strubell who was the innocent cause of the plight of Nick Ribsam. While he and Rickard were talking of nothing in particular, by the camp fire, hundreds of miles away, the cowboy indulged in a little quiet boasting about the two youths who were his companions. He represented them as sons of wealthy parents, who allowed them to do as they chose, and they were now enjoying a vacation after their own hearts.

It was this statement that gave Rickard his idea before he left camp. He hated the sturdy Nick intensely enough to shoot him down at the first opportunity, but to do that would intensify the anger against him, while it could do him no good, except so far as the satisfying of his revenge went; but if he took the boy to one of his safe retreats, he might force a good round sum from his rich parents to secure his safety.

The scheme savored strongly of the style of doing business in classic Greece, but you need not be told that it has been carried to a successful issue more than once within these glorious United States of America.

CHAPTER XXVII.

WATCHING AND WAITING.

THE presence of the Apaches within a short distance of the building brought about a complication for which the rescue party were as unprepared as were the whites within the structure. But for them, one of Nick's friends would have ridden forward and opened a conversation with Rickard, by which the terms of the exchange could have been effected with little delay. Herbert told Strubell that unless the criminal demanded an exorbitant price, it should be accepted. Although he had only a small amount of funds with him, he would give him a draft that would be honored without question by Mr. Lord in San Antonio; and if Rickard kept his part of the agreement, it would be respected by Herbert and his companions, who were governed by a sense of honor that would prevent any advantage being taken of circumstances that must of necessity be in their favor.

But if one of the party advanced to open communication, he would be observed by the watchful Apaches before a safe point was reached. Since Rickard must know of the presence of the red men, it was likely he would admit such an applicant the moment he saw his danger, but a sudden dash of the warriors might shut him out from the refuge.

The man would not allow the whole party to enter, inasmuch as that would disarrange his own plans, though he was not apt to object to the visit of one of their number. As yet, he could not have learned that the white men were behind the elevation of the prairie.

The simple question, therefore, was as to how Strubell and his companions could negotiate with Rickard without betraying themselves to the Apaches. Furthermore, it must not be forgotten that the situation of the three men and boy was extremely dangerous. They were on the open prairie, and liable to be discovered by the red men, even with the exercise of the extremest care on their own part. Such discovery was almost certain to be followed by a desperate fight, with the chances overwhelmingly against our friends.

This will be conceded when it is remembered that Geronimo and his fierce miscreants, who defied our forces in the South-west so long, never numbered more than a fractional part of the white soldiers. Those Apaches are born fighters, and the most dangerous Indians that ever trod the American continent. A dozen of them, well mounted, would make short work of three white men and one boy, no matter how bravely they might defend themselves. Eph Bozeman and the Texan friends were sure to do well and would tumble more than one of their assailants from the saddle, but their own ultimate destruction was inevitable.

The situation being as I have shown, it will be seen that the presence of the Apaches immeasurably increased the peril. It was agreed that no movement should be made until nightfall, up to which time the main object would be to avoid discovery by the swarthy raiders.

This was so important that Strubell and Lattin made their way back to where the ponies were grazing, and forced all of them to lie down. The four were so well trained that they readily obeyed. They would keep that posture, though suffering from hunger, until ordered to rise. There was no water within reach, a deprivation which the men felt as much as did the animals.

It should be stated that the words of Strubell about the plans of Bell Rickard gave Herbert a reasonable explanation of the course of Nick Ribsam, which, until then, was as much of a puzzle as the conduct of his captors. Doubtless he had been convinced from the words and action of his party that his life was not in immediate danger, and he therefore refrained from increasing their enmity by any attempt at escape. Had a good chance presented, he would have been quick to take it, but he was carefully watched and he bided his time.

Returning from the animals, the Texans lay down on the grass beside Herbert and Bozeman, and resumed watching the Apaches, with an occasional study of the front of the building for signs of the party behind the walls.

The Indians remained grouped in close order for nearly half an hour. Then one of their number galloped off for a hundred yards or more, circled about, and returned. Shortly after, a couple did the same thing.

"Do you know what that means?" asked Eph of Herbert.

"I have no idea."

"It doesn't mean nothin'; it's hard for a redskin to set still, though he can do it for hours at a stretch when he sees a chance of lifting any ha'r. Them chaps, and their ponies too, get tired of stayin' in one spot, so they take a little spurt like that to set thar blood goin'. Thar they go again!"

The party broke apart, and soon the whole company were circling about and back and forth like a lot of equestrians in a circus ring. They doubled in and out, in the most bewildering fashion, but the men, who devoted themselves to watching them closely, agreed that there were about a dozen, as at first supposed.

These exhibitions of horsemanship were of special interest to the party lying down behind the elevation, for the Apaches needed not to extend their circling far to pass behind the ridge, when they would be sure to discover them. And just about that time, as Strubell expressed it, the band would begin to play.

The red men rode so far to the eastward more than once that this discovery seemed inevitable. It caused much anxiety, and our friends withdrew their attention for a time from the building and kept it upon their more active enemies.

The situation was peculiarly trying to Herbert Watrous, who understood his danger in case of an attack from the Apaches. He would be perilously placed because of his inexperience. In fact, it struck him more than once that Nick had much the better of it as compared with him.

The one fortunate thing was that the afternoon was near to its close, and the night must lessen the danger, so far as the Apaches were concerned.

The latter were acting out their ferocious nature. When they knew the adobe building was empty, it possessed no attraction to them. They passed it by without so much as firing a shot at its gray walls, but, when they saw three horsemen ride through the broad entrance, they halted, and began laying their plans for destroying them. That's Apache nature, but perhaps, after all, it is not so different to the nature of the white man.

It was decided by the Texans that Eph Bozeman should ride forward to meet Bell Rickard. His relations with the horse thieves insured against the distrust they were likely to feel in the case of either of the others. He would doubtless be admitted without misgiving, and once within the building, he could complete arrangements for the ransom of Nick Ribsam.

It was Eph's choice to go on foot, though in the event of detection by the Apaches his case was likely to be hopeless, whereas, if he were mounted on his fleet plug, he might dash off and escape.

That which decided the old trapper was the

greater liability of being discovered if he rode a horse. The Apaches were certain to manœuvre about the building in the darkness, searching for a way of making a stealthy inroad on the defenders, and it was too much to expect them to fail to see a horseman seeking entrance through the regular avenue. Instead of walking erect, he would creep on his hands and knees, from the moment he reached the rim of the danger circle until he knocked at the door. By this course, though it involved much delay, he could use his marvellous expertness, trained to the highest point by a half century among the wilds of the Great West.

Old Eph had done the same thing before. He and Kit Carson once crept a full mile, over the cactus plains in Southern California, to elude a band of Navajoes that had followed them for several days and nights, and the injuries received during that ordeal were felt for months afterward.

He was glad of the chance to repeat the difficult feat, for he had lived an adventurous life too long to lose his liking for it, now that he was growing old. Besides, such persons are unwilling to admit any failure of their powers until the proof is forced upon them so impressively that it is impossible to deceive themselves.

CHAPTER XXVIII.

THE SOUND OF A PISTOL.

JUST as night was closing in, an occurrence took place which caused our friends more alarm than anything during the day.

Their position was almost due east of the adobe building, which it will be remembered was about a mile distant. The Apaches, who had been circling about on their ponies in an aimless way, drew nearer the building, until in the gathering gloom they were seen to be only a few hundred yards' distant.

Suddenly one of their number dashed off with his horse on a dead run to the east. He did not take a course toward the whites, but aimed for the elevation which extended in a southerly direction. It looked as if he meant to learn whether any friends of the little garrison were in the neighborhood.

"If he goes over the ridge," said Strubell in

a low tone, as all eyes were fixed on him, "he must see us."

He did not pass over, but halted at the top and sat motionless on the bare back of his pony, evidently engaged in scanning every portion of the visible prairie. At this moment old Eph glanced at the animals, a short way behind them, and saw that his horse was in the act of rising. His forequarters were up, and his head raised, after the manner of his kind, when his master spoke sharply and he immediately sank back again.

The action of the steed was as singular as it was unfortunate, and for a minute everyone was sure the discovery had been made. But the action of the Apache to the south left the matter in doubt. He wheeled about and rode back to his comrades at an easier pace, but they did not gather around him, as they would have been quite sure to do if he had borne important news to them.

The result was that neither Bozeman nor the Texans knew whether the Apache had seen them or not—a state of doubt as trying as actual discovery.

The belief was that the action of the horse had not betrayed them, for, until the red men faded from view in the deepening gloom, nothing to show the contrary was observable.

The night promised to be favorable for the dangerous enterprise. It would be quite dark, the moon not appearing until late, there was no wind, and, in the stillness, the slightest sound could be heard for a long distance. If the Apaches knew nothing of the party behind the elevation, they would be likely to remain on their horses, whose tread could be detected long before they were visible, while the advance of old Eph was to be in such utter silence that even the wonderfully fine hearing of an Apache would avail him naught.

"I'm goin' to start soon," said the trapper, "and I want to know what's to be said to Bell, if I get the chance to talk with him."

"In the first place," said Strubell, by way of reply, "Herbert is to fix the price of the ransom he's willing to pay."

"What do you think I ought to give?" asked the youth, who had thought a good deal over the question.

"I don't know—but it seems to me that a thousand dollars should be the outside figure. What do you think, Baker?"

"Five hundred is my idea, but I wouldn't think of goin' above what you say."

"Why," said the surprised Herbert, "I had fixed five thousand as the limit, not knowing but that I might exceed that."

"Don't think of it."

"Five thousand dollars," repeated old Eph, with a low whistle, for the sum to him was a prodigious fortune.

"Well, Eph can figure as best he can, but I will agree that that sum shall be paid, if Rickard will take nothing less."

"How are you goin' to pay it? What are the tarms?" asked the trapper, who knew nothing about the forms of "exchange," as it was proper to term the business in view.

"You can say to him that, if he will send Nick and his horse back to us unharmed, I will give him a draft on Mr. Lord in San Antonio for whatever sum you agree upon. He will understand that. I have the blanks with me, and can fill them in with pencil, which is as legal as ink. Then all he has to do is to hand the paper to Mr. Lord, who will give him the money without question. I will let him have another piece of writing which will insure that."

It was all a mystery to the old trapper, who had never seen anything of the kind, and perhaps there would be more difficulty in the way than the hopeful Herbert believed, but it was the best that offered, and since Rickard must, of necessity, be compelled to trust the others to a certain extent, he was not likely to propose other terms.

The matter was made clear, so far as could be done, to Eph, who, to insure he was right, repeated his instructions until they were pronounced correct by the others. Strubell, having some education himself, helped to force the bit of knowledge into his brain.

"S'pose he says he won't do it for five thousand, but wants six, or seven, or more—what then?" asked Eph.

"Make the best bargain you can; I am willing you should go up to six, seven—yes, ten thousand," added Herbert, who felt in that moment that there was nothing too much for him to do for the best friend he had in the world.

"Are you crazy?" asked the amazed Strubell. "What are you talking about?"

"I'm in earnest," was the resolute reply of the youth, who shuddered at the thought that a little haggling at the crisis might bring about the death of Nick Ribsam.

"Well," said the Texan, "since you talk that way, you can set it down as certain that Bell Rickard will turn Nick over in a hurry."

"Yas," added old Eph, "and go into the bus'ness of stealin' younkers instead of hosses, for it will pay him much bigger."

"But there's one thing you can work in," remarked Lattin, "that is, that he won't have any trouble in gettin' any sum up to five thousand, but when you go above that, there's sure to be difficulty and he may lose the whole thing."

All agreed that this was a clever idea which would have weight with the horse thief. The trapper promised to make the best use of it.

There seemed to be nothing more to settle, and Eph was ready to start.

"I'm goin' straight for the front of the buildin'," he said, "for the chance is as good on one side as t'other, but it will take me a good while to git thar."

"Suppose you run into trouble," suggested Strubell, "you must make a break for us and we'll do what we can for you."

"I won't do nothin' of the kind," was the reply of the trapper, "for that would be the last of you; I've got to go under some time, and what difference whether it's sooner or later? If the varmints jump onto me, I'll make the best fight I kin, but I don't want any of you foolin' round; all you need to do is to look out for yourselves and leave me alone."

It was useless to argue with old Eph, and no one tried to do so. After all, he was more likely to be right than wrong, though it seemed cruel to remain idle when he was in extremity.

"Wal, I'm off," he said, rising to his feet and striding down the slope toward the building.

As he did so he formed a striking figure. He loomed up large and massive in the gloom, with his long rifle grasped in his left hand, and his right resting on the revolver which he carried in the girdle about his waist. He took long steps, for he was so far from his destination that it was too soon to creep, but as his moccasins pressed the grass, not one of those watching him heard any sound. The progress of a shadow across the wall could not have been more silent.

The huge form quickly melted into the gloom, and all was still. Not once had the Apaches given utterance to their whoops, and they were so distant that the sounds of their horses' hoofs could not reach the watchers, a fact which the latter took as proof that the warriors had not discovered their presence on the elevation.

The minutes that followed were trying. The Texans knew that a long time must elapse before the trapper would reappear, even if the circumstances were favorable; in fact half the night was likely to pass ere he would show up again.

As nearly as they could judge, an hour had gone, during which the same profound quiet held reign, when all were startled by the sharp crack of a pistol from the direction taken by the trapper.

"What I feared!" whispered Lattin; "he's in trouble!"

CHAPTER XXIX.

THROUGH THE NIGHT.

WHILE Herbert Watrous lay on the ground, at the top of the elevation, with the Texans waiting for the return of the old trapper, he asked Strubell to explain their action on the night of the first norther, when they sent him and Nick through the hills to the other side.

"Well," replied the cowboy, "our first purpose was to have you out of the way when the scrimmage took place, for we knew it was coming sure."

"But you said you had no trouble with Rickard and his gang."

"And we didn't; off in another direction was a party of Comanches that must have taken us for their own warriors, for they began signalling in a way that made it look so. We answered their signals, but they found out the trick before we could trap them. However, they were out for game, and they came at us in the evening. It isn't worth while to give the particulars," added the Texan significantly, "but when the fun opened it wasn't long before the red gentlemen found out their mistake. They rode off—that is, some of them did—and that was all."

"But what of Rickard and his men?"

"While we were having the row with the Comanches they played a clever trick on us. They got round through the ridge, without our suspecting it till next morning, and walked off with Nick."

"They might as well have captured both of us," said Herbert, "and I have often wondered that they did not."

"They took the highest priced one," observed Strubell, with a chuckle, "but I guess there was another reason. Bell had a spite against Nick, and meant to put him out of the way if he couldn't fix the ransom business. While the main thing was money with him, it wasn't that alone."

This point in the story was reached when the three heard the report of old Eph's pistol, which rang out on the night with startling distinctness. It was nearer the building than the elevation where the friends were awaiting the return of the trapper.

"By gracious!" exclaimed Strubell in an excited undertone, "I can't stay here, knowing he needs our help, for all he told us to do so."

"And I feel the same way," added Lattin, rising partly to his feet, "but what about leaving Herbert here?"

It was this thought that held the two for a moment, but the youth hastened to say:

"If you can do him any good, go at once; I am in no danger."

"I think not, but I aint sure. If anything disturbs you," added the elder, "mount your horse and make off; your pony can go as fast as any of theirs."

But for the belief, confirmed by the action of the Apaches, that they did not suspect the presence of the whites, neither Strubell nor Lattin would have allowed Herbert to be alone; but they knew that if they were to help the trapper not a second was to be lost.

Instead of mounting their animals, they hurried down the slope on foot, breaking into a run, or rather loping trot, which enabled them to cover much ground with little noise, as their feet pressed the greensward.

The distance was considerable, and when they approached the spot where the pistol had been fired, they slackened their pace, listening and peering into the gloom, which was so deep that they could see no more than fifty feet in any direction.

"This must be near the place," whispered Lattin, "but where is he?"

"It's a good sign if we can't find him, though I don't understand why he used his pistol unless he was in trouble."

As nearly as they could judge, they were within two or three hundred yards of the building. It was so easy to err as to the point whence the report had come that they paused, undecided what to do.

Darkness was on every hand. Not the first outlines of the structure could be distinguished, nor was there a glimpse of any man or animal. The stars were shining brightly in the clear sky, and their light was all that guided their progress.

"We'll go a little further," said Strubell in the same guarded undertone, "but we must be on the watch, for we're in a bad place ourselves."

"*Sh!*" At that moment, they caught the sound of a horse's hoofs, their experience telling them the animal was on a gallop. The noise was faint—quickly dying out, thus showing that the pony was receding instead of approaching. Nothing, therefore, was to be feared from the rider of that particular animal.

To guard against passing their friend, the Texans now separated a few paces, taking care to keep within sight of each other. They pushed forward at a moderate walk, on the alert for the first evidence of danger.

A couple of rods were traversed in this manner when Lattin, who was on the left, emitted a faint hissing sound. At the same instant he sank to the ground, and Strubell was hardly a second behind him in doing the same. He saw nothing, but he knew that his friend did.

A form so dim, shadowy, and indistinct that he could trace nothing more than its outlines took shape in the gloom itself, a short distance in front of Lattin, who was so quick to utter the warning to his companion. It was not a horseman, but a man on foot.

The suspicion that it might be the trapper caused the Texan to give another faint call—so faint indeed that the alert ear of an Apache would not have noticed it. Old Eph would be sure, however, to read its meaning.

But the reply was not satisfactory. Instead of answering it with a similar signal, the silence was not broken, and, while the Texan was peering into the darkness, he became aware that he was staring at vacancy. The form had melted into the gloom—proof that it was moving in another direction.

"It must have been one of the varmints," whispered Lattin, as he stepped noiselessly to the side of his friend, "but I didn't s'pose they was walkin' round instead of ridin' their animals."

"They must suspect something; I guess Eph got through, after all."

"We'll go a little further," said Lattin, turning to the left again; "maybe he's hurt so bad he can't help himself."

The stillness continued, until once more they came together with the decision to return to the elevation where they had left Herbert. The fact that the Apaches were moving about on foot caused uneasiness concerning him, and they thought it best to return at once.

"Do you see it?" asked Strubell.

"Yes; we're further along than I thought."

It was the old mission building to which they alluded. It loomed to view in the darkness, its outlines dimly traceable against the starlit sky beyond. Not the first glimmer of a light showed, nor could the strained ear catch the semblance of a sound. But for that glimpse of the man on foot they would have believed the Apaches had departed with the coming of night.

It was idle to stay longer, and they turned about, moving off with the same care displayed from the first, for they were more anxious than either would confess to rejoin the youth, further away than they wished was the case.

The result of their venture did much to relieve them of fear concerning Eph Bozeman, though it was not altogether satisfactory. He might have collided with several Apaches on foot, and been despatched. It was impossible in the darkness to strike the exact spot where the meeting occurred, and, for aught they knew, the body of the old trapper was lying at that moment, cold and lifeless, with the face upturned to the stars.

As the distance from the building increased, the Texans hastened their footsteps, and it was a striking proof of their skill in such delicate situations that they came back to the elevation within a rod of the spot where they had left it. Without anything to guide them, except that strange, unexplainable intuition or instinct, this was a remarkable exploit in its way.

But to their alarm, when they peered about them, after recognizing the place, they failed to see Herbert.

"Something must have alarmed him," said Strubell; "but I hope it was nothing serious."

"We'll soon know," said Lattin, who moved hastily back to where the horses had been placed. He was away but a moment when he came back.

"The ponies are all there but his; he's gone."

CHAPTER XXX.

A FIGURE IN THE DARKNESS.

FOR the first time since joining the Texans in the pursuit of Bell Rickard and his captive, Herbert Watrous found himself entirely alone. He was lying on his face in the grass, at the top of the elevation, peering out in the night, and watching and listening for signs of friends and enemies.

It was not until the Texans had been gone several minutes that he began to fancy his own situation was threatened with the same peril that had overtaken Eph Bozeman, the trapper.

"They were never certain the Apaches didn't find out we were here," he thought, "and they may have been wrong in thinking that warrior did not observe us. If those people are as cunning as I have been told, who can say that their actions were not meant to throw two such experienced hunters as Strubell and Lattin off their guard?"

This was figuring matters to a fine point, and the result was that Herbert reasoned himself into a most uncomfortable frame of mind before his friends had been absent a quarter of an hour.

"I have half a mind to go out and mount Jill," he added, "and move off somewhere else; I would do it if the chances were not that I would ride into a worse place than this—my gracious!"

He was looking in the direction of the mission building, when something assumed form in the darkness immediately in front. Like the figure that caught the notice of Lattin at about the same time, the outlines were so indistinct that he could not identify it at first, but, with amazement and alarm, he speedily saw that a horseman had halted at the foot of the slope, with the face of himself and steed turned toward him. They were as motionless as if carved in stone, and their approach had been accompanied with no sound that reached the ear of Herbert.

There was something so uncanny in the apparition that, after first identifying it, the youth suspected it was a mistake, and that something affected his vision. He turned his gaze away, and even looked behind him. The result was similar to that which is noticeable when we gaze at the Pleiades on a clear night. Keen scrutiny shows but six stars, one modestly withdrawing before our ardent gaze, to reappear when we glance carelessly in the direction again.

Bringing back his eyes from their groping, Herbert saw the horseman so plainly that no room for doubt remained. He was there at the foot of the slope, apparently staring upward in the darkness with the same intensity that the lad was studying him.

There was no room for hoping that this stranger was a friend, for none of them had left the spot with his animal. It followed, therefore, that he was an Apache out for mischief, since that was the only errand that ever took those miscreants abroad.

"I believe it is the same one that rode to the top of the elevation just before night," thought Herbert; "he saw enough to know something is wrong, and is now seeking to find out for himself. He mustn't interfere with me," added the youth, compressing his lips, as he brought his rifle round in front.

Had the Apache made a charge upon him, Herbert would have let fly without an instant's hesitation. He was inclined to fire as it was; but, like the manly boy that he had become, he shrank from doing that which looked so much like a crime. Villainous as were the red men, he could not force himself to shoot one down in so heartless a fashion.

Besides, there was the possibility that the Indian did not know that anyone was on the elevation. Indeed, it might be said that the very appearance as described was evidence that he lacked such knowledge, for he had placed himself in a peril which one of his tribe would be sure to avoid. Herbert therefore decided to await more positive evidence of wrong intent before making any movement against the fellow.

His heart gave a quick throb when he discovered that the horseman was advancing. He heard the sound of his pony's hoofs, followed by a more distinct outlining of both.

"I do believe I shall have to drop him," thought Herbert, "and I wouldn't wait any longer if I wasn't afraid that it would bring the rest to the spot."

It was this fear that restrained him. There were likely to be others near who would swarm thither at the report of his gun, and more than likely make him prisoner, or slay him before he could leap into the saddle and dash off.

Self-interest urged him to wait until the last moment.

He reasoned that it was impossible for the sharp-eyed warrior to see him, since he was still flat in the grass; he must have possessed wonderful acumen to make his way to the spot in the darkness.

"It all depends on *you*," was Herbert's decision; "if you keep your distance no one will be hurt, but one step more and there will be a missing Apache."

The action of the latter was singular, for, after advancing a brief space, he again checked his pony and stood as motionless as before.

Nothing was clearer than that something was suspected at least by the red man to cause him to act in this manner. It may have been that his pony was the suspicious one, and the rider was debating with himself whether to explore further or give it up.

Undoubtedly it was fortunate for himself as well as for Herbert that he did not take long to reach a conclusion. At the moment the youth believed a meeting was certain, his steed wheeled and was off like a shot in the darkness—gone before Herbert could have taken any aim.

He drew a sigh of relief at being left alone once more and so unexpectedly.

"I believe that warrior will be back," was his conclusion, "and if he is he won't find *me* here."

Recalling the advice of Strubell, he hurried to where the horses had been left. They seemed to have concluded that the coming of night released them from the command of their masters to remain on the ground, for the whole four were on their feet, cropping the grass. Their saddles were in place, but their bits had been shifted to allow them to eat, and each one was improving his time.

Jill gave a faint whinny on recognizing his master, and seemed pleased to feel him in the saddle again.

"I don't know which way to go now that I'm ready," thought Herbert, "but it won't do to ride far, or Strubell and Lattin will have another young man's ransom to arrange for."

Manifestly the counsel of his friends was meant that he should hold himself ready to flee the instant it became necessary, but until then, the chances were even that he would not decrease his peril by a change of quarters.

A creditable motive led Herbert to adopt what might be called a compromise, and which was not lacking in a certain acuteness.

If he remained until detected by the Apaches, and should then dash off, they were sure to discover the other horses, and would shoot or stampede them, leaving the three men in a hapless plight; but if Herbert were charged upon at some other point, even if not

A FIGURE IN THE DARKNESS. 273

far removed, the animals might be overlooked in the flurry of pursuit.

He therefore rode his pony parallel with the elevation and in a southern direction, until he had gone a hundred yards or more, when he drew up, and awaited the development of events.

He did not go to the top of the slight ridge, but near enough to peer over without showing anything more than the head of himself and Jill.

All this time he did not forget the risk that would be run by getting too far from his friends. If they were to be troubled by trying to reunite with him, the complication was likely to affect Nick Ribsam as well. To prevent himself going astray, he therefore held along the ridge. That could not fail to be a sure guide to him whenever he wished to retrace his steps, for he had only to follow its course in reverse to reach the former place in a brief space of time.

His position now was quite similar to that of the Apache a short while before, for he was motionless on his steed, facing the top of the ridge, and waiting, watching and listening for whatever might come.

"The whole party of Apaches," he said to himself, "may be stealing toward this spot, thinking to find us all within their reach."

CHAPTER XXXI.

THE RETURN.

HERBERT was quite sure the Texans would not be gone long, unless they, too, became involved in a fight with the dusky raiders and shared in the probable fate of Eph Bozeman. If such proved to be the case, there would be sounds of the conflict, which would be as brief as it was desperate, and it was those for which he listened while sitting in his saddle on the slope.

The stillness remaining unbroken, he turned his pony toward the point he had left, and found, on reaching it, that Strubell and Lattin had arrived a few minutes before and were becoming anxious over his absence.

It was now a question whether the three should stay where they were or go elsewhere with their animals. The Apaches were prowling around the surrounding country so closely that it looked as if they had located the group.

Such was the view of Strubell and Herbert, but Lattin, on the other hand, was so positive that their enemies knew nothing of their presence that the others agreed to stay where they were until something more certain became known.

Trouble was likely to follow a change of base, since the trapper on his return would be puzzled to find them, though the Texans would be sure to give him all the help they could, and that was considerable.

There was nothing therefore to do but to wait, the most wearisome occupation of anyone. The nerves of all were strung to such a high point that there was little inclination to sleep. It was a long time since they had eaten or drank, and they were in need of food and drink, but no step was to be taken for the procurement of either until the momentous question was settled.

Lattin believed that the Indian horseman seen by Herbert received no inkling of the truth. His pony had detected something, and his rider, bringing him to a halt, sat looking and listening for the explanation that did not come. Concluding it was some wild animal or reptile moving in the grass, he had dashed off to join his companions.

Inasmuch as both the Texans were in accord by this time in the theory that they were not discovered by the red men, at the time of the scare just before sunset, the youth felt no fear in that regard. It followed therefore that the Apaches were unaware of their presence, and were not likely to learn of it except through some accident.

No one could forecast the result of the pistol shot that had rung out over the prairie, and which showed that the trapper's stealthy journey to the building had not been without incident.

The little company spoke only at intervals, and then in whispers. Their eyes and ears were so intently engaged that conversation interfered. The stillness was so profound that the champing of the horses was heard as they cropped the grass, while the sound of the hoofs was so distinct when they shifted about, that it seemed to Herbert they must draw the Apaches to the spot.

By and by one of the ponies stopped eating and lay down, then two others did the same, but the fourth kept it up so long that Lattin was about to go out and compel him to retire to his couch, when he did so. This left the quiet so perfect that it would have taken a wonderfully skilful warrior to steal up undetected on foot, and it was impossible for a horseman to do so.

The stars twinkled from a sky that was unclouded except in the western horizon, where a bank of clouds climbed part way to the zenith and shut out a portion of the faint light. In whatever direction the watchers gazed was the same blank darkness. Though they knew that men were near and constantly in motion, no glimpse of them was obtained.

"Baker," said the elder Texan in his guarded undertone, "I'm going to sleep for half an hour."

"All right," replied his companion; "I'll do the same when you wake up."

Strubell made not the slightest change in his position. He simply turned his head sideways upon his arm, bent at the elbow, and shut his eyes. Almost at the same moment he became unconscious.

The party had not removed their blankets from the backs of the ponies, through fear that it might delay them whenever a sudden movement should become necessary. They were stretched at full length on the grass. In that salubrious country, with its pure, dry air, there was no thought of ill results therefrom.

Herbert was near Lattin, and he asked:

"Will he wake at the end of the half hour?"

"If he don't I'll wake him," replied the other; "but I never knew Ard to vary more'n a minute or two."

"What do you make of Bozeman's long absence? Several hours must have gone by."

"It seems later than it is, but I expected him back before this."

"How do you account for his delay?"

"There may be several causes," replied Lattin; "in the first place, maybe he run into a hornets' nest and was knifed before he could shoot a second chamber of his revolver. Them Apaches work quick at such business, and they would shove Eph under in the style of greased lightning."

"But," suggested Herbert, who was after every grain of comfort, "it might be he found trouble in getting inside the building."

"That's likely, though Ard and me went up in sight of it without runnin' agin any of the varmints; but it couldn't have kept him all this time, for if he didn't get inside long ago he would have given up and come back to us."

"Do you suppose there has been any trouble with Rickard?"

"I don't see what trouble there could be; all the work Eph had was to find out the best the scamp would do, and then either agree or disagree with him. The most likely trouble is that Eph found the varmints so plentiful when he started to come back that he hasn't been able to get through and is waiting for the chance."

"If that proves the case, what will be done in the morning?"

"It's hard to tell till the morning comes. Rickard and Slidham may come out to help us fight our way in."

The incident was not impossible, but what a unique state of affairs it suggested! It recalled the affairs in the South-west, during the Mexican War, when a party of Comanches and "Greasers" would assail a handful of Americans, working as the most ardent allies until the Americans were disposed of, when the Mexicans and Indians would turn upon each other like cat o' mountains.

"Hello!" said Lattin a few minutes later, "there's the moon."

The upper edge of the gibbous orb was creeping above the horizon, and looked like the point of a fiery spear as it climbed rapidly upward.

"That's going to give us help," said Herbert, watching the satellite, whose ascent was strikingly swift.

"I don't know about that," replied the Texan; "it will let us see further 'cross the prairie, but don't forget that it'll do the same for the varmints. It won't be so easy for Eph to get back as it was to go forward, always providin' that he *did* go forward."

Strubell slumbered as quietly as an infant.

His breathing could not be heard, even in the perfect stillness which reigned. Herbert glanced at him more than once, with an odd fear that perhaps he was dead, but that was hardly possible.

Knowing the direction of the building, Lattin and Herbert tried to peer through the gloom and see it, but the light was insufficient to show its most shadowy outlines.

"Baker," whispered the youth, "I think I see something out there toward the building."

"Whether you do or not," replied the Texan, "I'm sure *I* do; someone is comin' this way."

"It must be an Apache."

"Keep quiet; we'll soon see."

As the hunter spoke, he made sure his rifle was ready to fire the instant it should become necessary. He was not troubled by the tender conscience of his companion in that respect.

The approaching figure was on foot, and, though advancing without noise, did so swiftly. It rapidly grew more distinct in the gloom, until the broad-brimmed hat, the massive frame, with the long rifle grasped in one hand, left no doubt of its identity.

It was old Eph Bozeman returning at last.

CHAPTER XXXII.

THE ENCOUNTER.

SUFFICIENT has been told to show that Eph Bozeman's stealthy approach to the mission building was attended by one stirring incident, if not more.

Leaving his comrades on the crest of the elevation, he strode forward at a rapid pace, until he had passed most of the intervening distance. Then he slackened his gait and crouched low, his body bent, until he resembled a person gathering himself for a powerful leap. This was his favorite posture when engaged upon such dangerous business, and he kept it until prudence told him there was too great a risk attending it.

His object was to defer creeping to the last moment, since his progress must become slower, but he was too much of a veteran to allow the question of convenience to detract from his vigilance.

At the point he had fixed in his mind he sank to the ground, and began using his hands and knees, not the most agreeable form of locomotion, since, as will be remembered, he carried his heavy rifle with him.

As yet he had seen and heard nothing of the Apaches, but believed a brush with them was inevitable before he could enter the building. He reasoned that since they knew of the presence of the white men inside, and were unaware of the others outside, they would devote themselves to circling about the structure, and maintaining a sharp lookout that none of the occupants got away during the night. The prospect of adding two or three more victims to the long list of massacres they had committed in the South-west was too tempting to be passed by, until all prospect of success was gone.

The trapper's belief was that the warriors would remain mounted, though he was too experienced to guide his own movements upon that theory alone.

So long as he kept his position close to the earth, he could discover the approach of a horseman before the latter saw him, to say nothing of the slight noise of the pony's hoofs, which was sure to betray him.

Twice he caught the latter sound, and ceasing his progress lay flat, listening and peering around in the gloom; but the riders did not come nigh enough for him to discern them; and after a brief wait he resumed his slow and laborious progress.

From what had taken place, he was absolutely certain that the Apaches had no suspicion that any whites were near the building. It followed therefore that no precaution had been taken against his approach, but they were vigilant enough to demand all the subtlety he possessed.

He was creeping forward in his guarded manner when, without the least warning, he saw the outlines of a figure in front, which, although dimly observed, he knew was one of the Apaches.

The trapper sank down again, with his keen eyes fixed on the warrior, who was standing with his back toward him, apparently studying the ground in the direction of the building, which was too far off to be seen, since Eph himself could not catch the most shadowy outlines of it.

Since the Apache had not observed the white man, there was no cause why he should do so, unless accident should lead him to face about. Without waiting a moment Eph began retreating, keeping his gaze on the red-skin, who faded almost from view in the gloom.

Then the trapper turned to the right and resumed his advance toward the building. Time was too valuable to wait for the Indian to shift his position, which, as likely as not, would prove unfavorable.

The flank movement was so regulated that he kept his enemy dimly in sight, for he did not mean to be surprised by any sudden action on his part.

All this was well enough, but the Apache overthrew the whole scheme by an unexpected movement.

The trapper was on his right, and a couple of rods distant, when the warrior seemed to conclude that it was time for him to do something. He stepped off at his usual pace, which would have carried him speedily beyond sight had Eph been somewhere else, but unfortunately he moved straight toward the old hunter.

To retreat or advance would have been certain betrayal, and Eph did not attempt it. Instead, he silently drew his pistol and grasped it, ready for firing.

The Apache had no thought of anything of this kind, but he had taken less than three paces, when he discovered the figure on the earth in front of him. He uttered no outcry, but stopped and placed his hand at his waist, as if to draw a weapon therefrom. He, too, carried a gun, most likely a Winchester, and was expert in its use. He had no blanket, his body being bare above the waist, and his long, coarse hair dangled about his shoulders. He was much shorter and smaller in every way than the white man, but every ounce of his body was like that of a tiger.

The Indian might have brought instant help by a signal, but to do that would have been a confession that he was afraid to attack a single individual, and the warrior "wasn't that sort of a fellow."

His pause was only momentary. He stooped down like an animal about to leap across a chasm and the trapper caught a movement of his right hand, which convinced him the warrior had drawn a knife and meant to spring upon him.

Eph's revolver was leveled at the savage, who was still stealing forward when a single chamber was discharged. The shot was unerring, and (what was singular in the case of an American Indian) he sank downward without any outcry.

The trapper needed no one to tell him what next to do. He knew the report of his weapon would bring nearly if not all the other Apaches to the spot, and he could not get away too soon. Springing to his feet, he loped swiftly toward the building, never pausing until he stood in front of the broad door.

He glanced keenly to the right and left while making this run, but though he heard the sounds of hoofs, he saw none of the raiders eager for the chance to cut him down.

Within a half minute after the shot was fired an Apache reached the spot on his pony, and was quickly joined by five others, all mounted. The prostrate figure told the story, but the author of their comrade's death was gone.

While one of them lifted the inanimate figure upon his steed, the others separated to find the white man who had slain him. They did this with rare skill, but they were misled from the start. Knowing nothing of those outside the building, their supposition must have been that one of them had stolen out of the structure and gained this point before discovery. It was not to be supposed that he was striving to enter instead of leave the place, and they therefore widened the circle, when they should have contracted it.

CHAPTER XXXIII.

IMPORTANT NEGOTIATIONS.

THE shot which the trapper fired in self-defence, therefore, was of the utmost help in his approach to the old mission building, for it broke the line of circumvallation, which otherwise would have been impassable to anyone seeking to enter or leave the structure.

To this also was due the escape of Strubell and Lattin when they hastened to the spot. It may be said that the entire plan of the Apaches was disarranged. In trying to cover so extensive a circle, they left of necessity vast gaps, through which the Texans passed without detection. It must have been one of the Apaches engaged in this curious hunt that approached Herbert Watrous, as he lay on the summit of the elevation awaiting the return of his friends.

The trapper did the best thing possible, for he had taken but a few steps when the outlines of the old mission house assumed form in the gloom, and he did not halt until he was at the door.

Despite the stirring incident through which he had just passed, none of them tried his nerve as did this last phase of his experience. He could not know how long he would be kept waiting; the Apaches were sure to appear shortly. If forced to stay for a brief period where he was, he must be discovered, and the position of a single man at bay in front of a building, without the liberty to enter, and obliged to meet the attack of a dozen enemies, need not be dwelt upon.

Eph gave the heavy door several violent kicks the moment it was within reach, and the sound could not only have been heard throughout the interior, but a long way beyond. The Apaches were sure to make a speedy investigation.

Fortunately for the trapper he was not kept long in suspense. Bell Rickard could not fail to hear the energetic summons, and quickly called from one of the upper windows, taking care not to expose himself:

"Who's there?"

"Me, Eph Bozeman."

"Where the mischief did *you* come from?" asked the criminal, now venturing to thrust his head from the window.

"Never mind whar I come from," replied the impatient applicant; "come down an' let me in powerful quick or you won't git the chance to let me in at all."

"All right! I'll be there."

It seemed a long while before Rickard descended to the door, during every second of which Eph expected the Apaches. He stood ready to let fly with rifle and revolver at the first sight, but, while waiting, he heard Rickard at the door, which was speedily unbarred, and he stepped inside more quickly than he had ever done anything of the kind before.

All was dark, but Rickard did not speak until he had refastened the door, which was composed of a species of carved wood, still seen in the old mission houses of the Southwest, which is hardly less strong and endurable than the adobe walls themselves.

The trapper was so familiar with the interior of the structure that he walked readily along the broad, open hallway, into the court beyond, where there was sufficient light to observe the figure of his companion as he led the way to a small apartment opening into the court, and within which a dim light was burning.

Into this the two passed, on the first floor, where Eph found himself face to face with Bell Rickard and Harman Slidham, whom he had met a short time before, and knew to be among the most lawless characters in the States and Territories.

"I was up in front of the building," said Rickard, "looking out for the Apaches when I heard you at the door."

"Yes," replied the trapper, "I tried to make you hear me."

The room which the three entered was one of a dozen similar ones, opening upon the court in the centre, the building forming what might be described as a hollow square. Many years before the apartment had probably been used as sleeping quarters by the fathers, who devoted their lives to labor among the Indians,

IMPORTANT NEGOTIATIONS.

who, it must be confessed, rarely showed any appreciation of their self-sacrifice.

It was twenty feet deep, and perhaps half as broad, without furniture, but with walls several feet in thickness. The only openings were the door and two narrow windows facing the court. These let in sufficient light to give all the illumination required during the daytime.

In the rear of this room Rickard kept his supply of meal and dried meat for such contingencies as the one that now seemed upon him. The door, of the same material as the main one, could be secured so that a forced entrance required great labor and effort, while the windows were too strait to allow the smallest person to squeeze his body through.

From an iron bracket in the wall burned an oil lamp which lit up the interior, showing the sacks of grain and a couple of boxes containing dried meat. The sacks and boxes furnished seats for the men during their conference.

The trapper glanced searchingly around, and was surprised to see nothing of Nick Ribsam, though he made no reference to it; but knowing of the supply of water, he asked for a draught before opening proceedings.

An earthen vessel contained a gallon or so, which Slidham had brought only a short time before from the spring near by. Eph quaffed long and deep before setting it on the rough floor, and drew the back of his hand across his mouth, with a sigh of enjoyment.

"You can't improve much on that," he remarked, resuming his seat on one of the bags of grain.

"No; it goes pretty well when you have been without anything for two or three days," replied Rickard, who suspected the errand that had brought his old acquaintance thither.

"It isn't as bad as that, but we haven't had a swaller sence crossing the Pecos to-day."

"You say 'we'; how is that, Eph? When we parted you were travelling the other way, and no one was with you."

"You're right on that, but I met Ard Strubell and Baker Lattin, who had a younker with 'em, and they war after you."

"After *me!* What was that for?"

"Come, Bell, none of that; you understand what it means; you've got a younker, and they want him."

"Are they willing to pay for him?" asked the horse thief.

"Wal, if you're mean 'nough to ask it, they're ready to give something, but, Bell, I hardly expected this of you; I knowed you war dealin' in hoss-flesh, but I didn't know you war goin' to start in this line of bus'ness."

Eph Bozeman was a man who spoke his mind under all circumstances, and he felt not the slightest fear of the couple, who had followed a life of outlawry for many years.

Slidham lit his pipe and listened. Rickard was the leader, and he was content to let him do the talking for the two. The evil fellow did not beat about the bush.

"It doesn't make any difference to me what you expected or didn't expect; you wouldn't have come here at this time unless it was on business, and if you've got anything to say to me there's no use in waiting."

"I guess mebbe your right, Bell: of course Ard and Baker know what you run off with the younker for; you mean to keep him till you get a reward for givin' him up."

"You've hit it the first time," replied Rickard.

"Wal, the boys talked it over, and they didn't like it much, but the younker with them says he's willin' to give somethin', but nothin' very big. How much do you want?"

"What are they willing to pay?"

"That isn't the way to hit it, Bell, name what you want, and if it's too big why I'll go back and tell 'em so, and they won't give it, that's all, but wait for a chance to even matters with you."

"What would they say to five thousand?" asked Rickard in a hesitating way which gave the cue to the trapper. He rose abruptly from where he sat on the sack of meal.

"Let me out the gate."

"What for?" asked the surprised criminal.

"When you talk that way, thar's no need of my waitin'."

"I asked you to name a sum, but you wouldn't."

"I didn't s'pose you war goin' to ask all the money thar is in New York," said the trapper, whose ideas of the financial resources of the great metropolis were crude.

"Well, make a proposal and I'll tell you what I'll do."

"Baker thought five hundred was plenty, but Ard said if you stuck out I might go a thousand."

"It's the other young man that pays it, isn't it?"

"Of course."

"What does *he* say?"

"Not much of anything," replied Eph, who saw the advantage he possessed and did not mean to let go of it.

"How is he going to pay the money? Has he got it with him?"

"Of course not; but he explained that he would give you a draft—I b'lieve they call it— that is, a piece of paper with writin' on it, which you can hand over to Mr. Lord in Santone, and he'll pay you a thousand dollars—which shows what a fool Mr. Lord is, for how can a piece of paper be worth anything like *that?*"

"You're asking me to trust them a good way," said Rickard, who had hoped that the parties would be able to produce the funds, "for they may get word to the banker and he won't pay it. Then I'll be out with no way to help myself."

"As I figger it," said the trapper, wrinkling his brow with thought, and anxious to display his knowledge, "thar aint no way of fixin' it without takin' a risk like that. You've knowed me and Ard Strubell and Baker Lattin for a good many years, and you know that when we give our promise we'll stick to it. Aint that so?"

"I don't dispute it."

"Wal, then, we three, includin' likewise the younker as is to pay the money, give you our promise that if you'll send this one with you back to them, with his hoss, gun, an' everything right, they'll give you that paper, which will bring you one thousand dollars the minute you hand it to Mr. Lord in Santone."

"That seems to be straight, though I ought to have more."

"I forgot to say that the younker said if

you should ask a big sum he couldn't save trouble in your gettin' it, which means, I s'pose, that he'll have to work it through New York, or somethin' like that, but thar won't be any trouble 'bout five hundred or a thousand dollars."

CHAPTER XXXIV.

A STRANGE DISCOVERY.

BELDEN RICKARD understood business customs much better than the simple-hearted trapper, though it will be admitted that the latter managed his part with cleverness. He had expected to agree upon a ransom of five thousand dollars at the least, and it has been shown that Herbert Watrous was willing, under stress, to advance double that sum for the release of his friend; but the amount was fixed at one thousand, which is far below the usual rates.

Rickard understood what Eph meant when he spoke of the trouble about arranging for the payment of a greater amount. Young Watrous had a credit to the extent named with Banker Lord of San Antonio, and to secure more he would have to consult with his parents in New York.

This meant delay, which he was anxious

above everything to avoid, since it involved personal danger to him. As it was, he dreaded presenting himself to so well-known a resident as the banker, but was thinking of turning over the draft to some trustworthy friend when Eph, recalling what Herbert had told him to say, added that the young man would give him a letter to Mr. Lord that would prevent the very trouble he feared.

This closed negotiations. Rickard accepted the terms and did a neat piece of diplomacy by saying:

"No matter how this is fixed I've got to trust you folks, so I will do it clear through; I'll send the boy back with you, and you can tell your friends to arrange it with the banker so that I'll get the money whenever I call or send someone, and no questions will be asked."

"I'll guarantee that that'll be done," was the emphatic pledge of the trapper, who not only meant every word, but knew there would be no withdrawal or deception on the part of his friends.

"But," added Rickard, who, strangely

enough, had overlooked one momentous fact, "what about the Apaches? Old Kimmaho and his gang are out there, and there's no saying when they'll go."

This was the most serious phase of the business. Old Eph had been speculating over it from the moment he left his companions on the elevation.

Now that the terms were agreed upon with the captors of Nick Ribsam, and they were ready to turn him over to his friends, how was he to be escorted back to them?

"Didn't you have trouble in getting here?" asked the criminal of the trapper.

"I had a little brush, and dropped one of the varmints."

"That, then, was your pistol that I heard?"

"I shouldn't wonder, bein' as I fired off a pistol while tryin' to make a call on you."

"If you had such trouble in slipping by the Apaches, you are sure to have a good deal more when the boy is with you. You know old Kimmaho, Eph?"

"I rather think so; he's as bad as Geronimo."

"Then when he has learned of what took place, he and his warriors will be more watchful than before."

"Thar can be no doubt of that," replied the trapper, with an impressive nod of his head; "I wouldn't be afeard to try it alone if thar war twice as many, but I won't be able to manage it with the younker."

"What shall be done?"

"You may shoot me if I know; I've been figgerin' over the bus'ness for the last hour and can't make nothin' of it."

But Rickard had a proposition to make. It was a singular one, but he was in earnest and would have kept his part as faithfully as he knew the other parties would keep their pledge.

"You can get back to Strubell and Lattin if you try it alone; do that, and then all of you come in here with me. I will be on the lookout so that you can dash right through the door as soon as you reach it."

The curious feature about this proposition is that while it was the most feasible that could be thought of, it displayed a certain chivalry on the part of the horse thieves, which would have struck anyone as inconsistent with the character of the one making it.

"It's the idea," said old Eph, after thinking it over for a few seconds; "now, if you'll fetch the younker so that I can have a few words with him, I'll be ready to start back; I'd like to be able to tell his friends that I seen him again and spoke to him."

"Of course," said Rickard, turning to Slidham and saying something in so low a tone that the sharp-eared trapper could not catch the words. The fellow, who had simply held his peace, smoked and listened, nodded his head, rose, and passed through the open door into the courtyard. Eph heard his footsteps on the adobe pavement, which had been trod and seasoned during the past century into a hardness like that of the walls themselves.

When the sounds died out the trapper threw a ponderous leg over the other, puffed at his pipe, and, looking across in the face of one of the most famous horse thieves in Western Texas, asked in his off-hand fashion:

"How's business, Bell?"

"Mighty bad," was the reply, accompanied by a shake of the head.

"How's that?"

"There are too many at it, and the officers are after us too sharp. You remember Zip Cooley?"

"I've knowed Zip for twenty years, but have lost track of him for the past two or three seasons. How is he?"

"He's at rest at last," replied Rickard, with another sigh. "The vigilantes down in Nacogdoches country got the drop on him—used him mighty mean—made him dance on nothing, with his chin among the limbs of a tree. Poor Zip was one of the best men I ever had, but he's crossed the big divide."

"That was bad for Zip," said Eph grimly, "but I don't reckon the folks down in Nacogdoches will rear a monument reachin' to the clouds to keep his mem'ry green."

"Then," added Rickard, "Waxhurst and Doffgo wanted to branch out, so they crossed over into Arkansas, made a good haul, and started through the Indian Nation."

"How did they make out?"

"Well, they 'branched out' the same as poor Zip; you see, our gang has been cut down pretty low, and when the rangers gather one in, there isn't enough at hand to rally, shoot the officers, and rescue him."

"What a blamed pity," growled the trapper, leisurely puffing his pipe, "that thar warn't enough of you just to clean things out atween El Paso and Santone."

"No; I wouldn't want it as good as that; but we ought to have enough to make it interesting, and give a fellow a chance to make an honest living. I had a pretty close call myself a couple of months ago."

"How was that?"

"It was over in the Panhandle; Slidham and me were alone, and they run us hot, but we tumbled the leader out of his saddle, hit the man next to him, and before they could get things in shape, slipped off in the moonlight."

"Isn't Slidham a long time bringin' that younker?" asked Eph, looking impatiently at the door.

"Yes—ah, here he is!"

The man appeared at that moment, his face showing that he was agitated over something. He gave Rickard an anxious look, and, without speaking, nodded his head in a way which signified something important.

"Eph, you'll excuse me for a few minutes," said the leader, hastily rising to his feet and moving to the door; "I won't keep you waiting long."

The couple passed out together and the trapper found himself for the first time entirely alone. He cared nothing for that, however, but continued slowly puffing his pipe, and wondering what the action of the others could mean.

Several times he heard them moving about the court, and when he was on the point of going to them, with a demand for an explanation, Rickard returned, hastily stepped within the apartment, and without sitting down looked earnestly at his visitor.

"Eph," said he, "don't you believe I'm playing square with you?"

"What put that ar silly question in your head? Of course I do."

"We agreed on the terms, didn't we?"

"That's just what we done."

"Well, the deal is off."

"What do you mean by such stuff?" demanded the trapper, unable to repress his astonishment. "Aint you satisfied with the tarms?"

"Of course, but I can't carry out my part; I can't deliver the goods."

"WHAT!"

"Nick Ribsam isn't in the building; he has escaped!"

CHAPTER XXXV.

THROUGH THE LINES AGAIN.

THERE could be no doubt of the truth of the startling declaration of Bell Rickard. He had no object in deceiving the trapper, for his failure to produce Nick Ribsam deprived him of the liberal ransom agreed upon by the representative of Herbert Watrous.

He stated that he had told his prisoner of the plan he had in view, so that the youth might be relieved of all dread of violence or harm, and could be content to abandon whatever plans he had in mind of escape. He assured him that, even if he succeeded in getting away, he would be in greater danger than ever, since the chances were against his finding his friends, while the Apaches were quite sure to find him.

Nick seemed to be impressed with this view, and Rickard and Slidham concluded that he meant to wait patiently for his release by the method explained to him. It now looked as if Nick had succeeded in outwitting his captors, after all, and that his apparent resignation was meant to deceive them into relaxing their watchfulness.

Although the two men and boy were observed by Kimmaho and his warriors as they rode up to the adobe structure, they were able to enter and secure the massive door before the Apaches could interfere. Rickard assured Nick that it was a fortunate thing for them, since they would have been badly caught but for the refuge, where they could laugh at the enmity of ten times that number of warriors.

If the criminal had felt any misgivings as to the intentions of Nick, they were removed by this time; for, after having refused all the chances offered him, who would suppose that he would place himself in the most imminent peril possible from the Apaches, when he had no knowledge that his friends were within a hundred miles?

Nevertheless he was gone. When Rickard found the trapper at the door, he asked Nick to remain in another part of the building until the interview was over. It struck him that it was better that he should not listen to the negotiations, though he was willing to bring him forward when asked to do so.

The criminal indicated no particular one of the dozen apartments opening on the courtyard, several of which were intended for the use of horses. The front of the building consisted of two stories, with four large rooms, but the other portion was only a single story in height.

When Eph asked for a few words with the boy, Rickard sent Slidham out to bring him in. The man expected to find him at once, but as he moved from one apartment to another, calling to him in a suppressed voice and hearing nothing in reply, he began to fear something was amiss. However, he completed the circuit, including the four large apartments in front and the room where they had placed their ponies.

Since he carried no light, it was easy for the youth to keep out of sight; but Slidham could think of no reason for his doing this, and he returned to his chief with the word that he believed the prisoner had "vamosed the ranch." Deeming it incredible, Rickard set out to make the search thorough. He carried no light, but was fully supplied with matches, and he burned several in each apartment, until he had scrutinized the entire interior, and made sure the youth had not fallen asleep or was hiding.

It so happened that the stables were the last place visited. Rickard was holding the tiny match above his head, anxiously awaiting the moment when its light should reveal the whole interior, when Slidham touched his arm, and, pointing at the ponies, whispered:

"There's only *two* of them!"

"You're right," replied the leader; "it's his horse too that is gone."

It was true: the faithful Jack that had stood by his master so long was not in sight. All doubt was removed, and Rickard hastened to where he had left Eph Bozeman and told the astounding news.

The criminal proved his earnestness by asking the trapper to help him in repeating the search, and he did so, visiting every room in the building, but without gaining sight of the missing youth.

"Great guns!" exclaimed Eph, "how did we come to forgit it?"

He started on a run for the main door. The others were at his heels, for they knew what the action meant. If Nick had stolen out and galloped off, he must have left the entrance open for anyone to enter. The instant the Apaches discovered it they would swarm through, for, as has been shown, the presence of the few white men within rendered them furiously eager to enter when otherwise they would have cared not at all.

Even such a veteran as Eph Bozeman shuddered on reaching the heavy doors to find them unfastened, so that a small child could have passed through from the outside with no trouble.

"If the varmints had only knowed that!" he said, after helping to secure it again.

This of course changed all the conditions and brought the men in front of a new and alarming problem. Since they were assured that Nick Ribsam, in spite of the danger from the Apaches, had ridden out of the front of the building, and his present whereabouts were unknown, beyond the simple fact that he was not present, Eph Bozeman felt that he could not get back to his friends too soon with the news, and decide upon an immediate line of action to help the rash youth.

Rickard renewed his proposal that the others should dash into the building and stay there until all danger passed. The Apaches would be certain to discover them in the morning if not before, and the three hunters and single youth could not maintain themselves against Kimmaho and his band.

This offer would have been accepted without hesitation, but for the desertion it forced of Nick Ribsam. The entire course of his friends for days past was with the single view of helping him, and it would not do to leave him now when his peril had been increased a hundredfold.

But admitting all this, the question rose, as to what possible way there was of aiding the young man, who had done that which Eph Bozeman could not understand, after hearing so much of his brightness.

Indeed, he more than half suspected that he had already fallen into the hands of the Apaches. His own passing of their lines was of the most difficult nature, as the reader has learned, and it looked impossible for it to be done a second time, and by one who knew so little of those subtle red men.

The fact that Nick was mounted ought to have been of great help in the event of discovery, for his pony was as fleet as the fleetest of the Apache steeds, but those ferocious raiders would find little trouble in entrapping the boldest white man who ventured within sight of them on so dark a night.

Be the conclusion what it may, the necessity of the trapper returning to the Texans was obvious. He told Rickard that he would try it at once, and no decision could be reached until after a talk with them.

"If we agree to make a break for these quarters, it'll be just as it is growin' light," said he.

"I'll be on the lookout," replied Rickard, "and you can feel certain there won't be any trouble in gettin' in."

With this understanding a careful survey was taken of the ground immediately in front, and, nothing being seen of the Apaches, the visitor stepped outside. He had spent several hours within the building, and knew his friends were wondering at his long absence, but he now did a thing for which there seemed no justification.

Fairly without the door, he moved aside a few paces, as if to leave, but instead of doing so, stood motionless, with his back against the outer wall. He was listening for something besides Apache warriors, and by and by he heard it; it was the noise made by Bell Rickard in refastening the heavy doors. He had waited until he believed his caller was gone too far to return, when he secured himself and companion against the common enemy.

The moment the door was locked Eph stepped noiselessly forward and stooped down. It was too dark for him to see distinctly, but he could feel as well as ever, and he passed his hands back and forth over the earth, as if he had lost a valuable coin and was searching for it through the sense of touch alone.

CHAPTER XXXVI.

THE DECISION.

THE situation of the trapper was perilous in the extreme, for it was to be supposed that the Apaches, after the loss of one of their number, would maintain unremitting watch of the only avenue through which anyone could enter or leave the building; but he remained in a stooping posture for several minutes, passing his hands back and forth over the ground, until he had several times covered the space in front of the door.

Finally, with a muttered exclamation, he stood erect, and was ready to start toward his friends, a long way off on the elevation where he had left them hours before.

His keen ear, trained to wonderful fineness by his years of life in the wilderness, caught the footfalls of a horse, which he knew at once was ridden by one of the Apaches. Instead of moving off, or attempting to re-enter the building, he remained upright, with his back against the structure. Had there been a corresponding figure on the other side of the door, a person observing the two from a brief distance would have declared they had been carved and set there scores of years before.

The Indian rode up within sight, and halted a moment while he gazed at the front of the structure. Nothing was easier than for the trapper to tumble him from his pony, but he was too wise to summon the band by doing so. He gazed at him in turn, content to let him alone as long as he did not disturb him.

The Apache must have felt that he was in danger of drawing a shot from one of the upper windows, for he quickly wheeled his steed and rode off in the darkness.

He was hardly out of sight when Eph moved straight out from the building. If Rickard or his companion were on the watch they must have wondered at the sight, though it was explainable on the ground that the trapper was waiting a favorable opening to run the gauntlet.

Instead of crawling, the veteran broke into

his loping trot, which was speedier than it appeared. The moon had risen, and though it was at his back he feared the result of the exposure to its additional light.

In no way can the success of Eph be explained other than on the ground that it was one of those pieces of extremely good fortune which sometimes attend rash enterprises on the part of a cool-headed man. He heard the sound of galloping horses, and twice caught their shadowy outlines, but he was on the alert, and, dropping to the earth, waited until the peril passed. In both cases the red men came no nearer, and he was soon advanced so far that he believed the worst was over. He straightened up once more, and, as I have shown, strode directly forward to the elevation, where all three of his friends were awaiting his coming with an anxiety that cannot be understood by one not similarly situated.

The little party listened to his story with breathless interest, Herbert being the first to speak at its conclusion.

"That's just like Nick," he said; "he has been waiting his chance all these days and nights, and when those men had no suspicion of what he intended, he has given them the slip."

"I don't have much opinion of *that* younker," said the old trapper curtly.

"Why not?"

"The most foolishest thing he could do was to ride out of that building just as it 'pears he has done. If he had stayed thar the whole thing war fixed, but now whar ar you?"

"If he has fallen into the power of Kimmaho or any of his party," said Strubell, "it will take more than a thousand dollars to get him back."

"What do you suppose they will demand?" inquired Herbert, his fears aroused again.

"They won't ask *anything*," said Lattin; "the Apaches don't deal in the ransom bus'ness as much as some other folks."

"But you talk as though he is a prisoner of theirs."

"If he is alive, what else can he be?"

"He was well mounted and might have escaped on horseback."

"If that had been the case," added the elder Texan, "we couldn't have helped knowing it."

"But there was no noise when Eph met the Apaches except the report of his pistol."

"We have been listening so closely here, except when I was asleep, that we noticed the tramp of the Apaches' ponies even when they were walking; if Nick rode off at full speed we must have heard the sounds, because they would have been much louder."

"Suppose on leaving the building, during Eph's interview with the two men, he had ridden around to the rear and galloped several miles to the westward, would you have heard Jack's hoofs?"

"Thar's somethin' in that," remarked the trapper; "you're all pretty sharp-eared, but that would have been too much for you to catch."

"The supposition, however, is a very thin one," insisted Strubell, to whom the action of Nick Ribsam was very annoying.

"I'm sorry he did it," remarked Herbert, "but we must take things as they are, and when we meet him we'll haul him over the coals."

"Did Bell know anything about our being out here?" asked Strubell, turning to the trapper.

"He 'spected you three, but he didn't know nothin' 'bout *me*, and didn't know when you would show yourselves. He s'posed I would meet you and give you the news, and you would hurry along. He knowed you war aimin' for the old mission buildin' and would be along after a while if the varmints didn't cut you off."

"What about our pack animals?"

"He spoke of 'em, and said Jim-John and Brindage would 'tend to 'em."

"You did so well in arranging the ransom that you ought to have included them."

"I could have done it if you had said so, but I follered orders," replied the trapper.

"Well," said Lattin, "the question now is what we are to do; if Nick only knowed where we are it would be simple enough; he could give the Apaches the slip and hang 'round till mornin', when we could come together."

"But it looks as if he will ride till daylight as hard as his pony can stand it—that is, if the redskins haven't got him," observed Strubell, "and we may hunt over the whole of New Mexico and Arizona without finding him."

"It don't seem to me that it will be as bad as that," remarked Herbert, eager to gather every crumb of comfort; "for he must know he can't find us by riding westward, but will start eastward after escaping the Apaches, so as to meet us on the way."

"But that start that you're talking about," reminded Strubell, "has been made hours ago, if it was made at all, and he must now be far to the eastward."

"He will be on the lookout for us and will strike the trail before going far."

"I see no reason to believe that; we are not following any trail at all; if we were there would be hope, but the chance of his finding our footprints equals that of picking up a certain blade of grass on the left bank of the Brazos, when no one can direct you within a hundred miles of the spot."

Herbert was trying to gather hope from the

different views of the situation, but it looked as if his friends were determined to prevent anything of the kind.

"If you folks knew Nick Ribsam as well as I," he sturdily insisted, "you would have a higher opinion of him than you seem to have."

"Baker and I thought as well of him as you," said Strubell, "but we are judging him now by what he did this evening; if he had stayed where he ought to have stayed the whole business would have been over."

"But the Apaches are still near us," replied Herbert.

"We could manage that; Rickard would let us inside, where we could all be together; Kimmaho might lay siege to us for days or weeks, but he couldn't harm us, and after a time would grow tired and ride off to more inviting fields."

"It looks to me," observed Lattin, who seemed to dislike the general condemnation in which he had joined of a youth of whom they had all become fond, "that the most that can be said about the younker is that he has made the same mistake that one of us was likely to make. He found what he thought was a good chance to give the scamps the slip, and he done it as neatly as anything of the kind was ever done in this world."

Eph Bozeman had held his peace for some time. Strubell now turned to him and asked his views, adding that they would be followed.

"All right," he replied decisively; "at the first streak of daylight to-morrer we make a break for the old buildin' yonder."

CHAPTER XXXVII.

THE FINAL CHARGE.

AT the earliest streaking of gray in the eastern horizon the three men and Herbert Watrous, all of whom had been sleeping fitfully by turns through the long dismal hours, silently rose to their feet and walked to where the ponies, a short distance off, had resumed their cropping of the grass. They were thirsty, like their masters, but no water was within reach, and they were doing their best to satisfy their hunger.

The outlines of the old adobe mission building showed faintly through the obscurity as the little party headed westward, and advanced at a moderate walk, on the alert for the Apaches, of whom they had detected signs now and then during their wearisome watching.

The action of the red men had puzzled the trapper as well as Strubell and Lattin. It was hard to understand why they had not stumbled on the truth, but there was good reason for believing they were still ignorant of the presence of the white men so near them. It was upon this theory that the success of the daring enterprise was based.

Eph Bozeman placed himself at the head, Herbert coming next, with one of the Texans on either side. The veteran was the best qualified to lead, while the disposition of all was with a view of protecting the younger and less experienced member of the party.

Nothing was seen of their enemies until half the distance was passed, when Lattin, who was on Herbert's right, exclaimed in an undertone:

"Yonder are the varmints!"

The horses were in excellent condition because of their long rest, and up to this moment moved at a moderate trot. As the Texan spoke, the trapper, who had detected the danger, struck his animal into a brisk gallop, the others doing the same without any urging of their riders.

The Apaches must have relaxed their vigilance toward the latter part of the night, for most, if not all the group, were observed to the south of the structure instead of being near it. They were closer to it, however, than the whites, and showed their daring by immediately riding forward to meet them.

The trapper turned his head and said: "Let 'em have it the minute they're near enough to hit."

These were words which had meaning, and Herbert, like his companions, looked at his Winchester to make sure it was ready for instant service.

"I think they're all there," added Lattin.

"I don't believe it," remarked Strubell, "for there isn't more than six or eight."

"And Nick isn't with them," Herbert could not help exclaiming, with a thrill of pleasure.

No reply followed this, which might signify nothing, for all were too intent on what was before them.

The interest deepened each moment. The Apaches, numbering exactly eight, were advancing at a speed fully as great as that of the whites, riding close together and apparently all eagerness for the conflict. They indulged in no shouts, whoops, or gestures, but came on like the grim demons they were.

Each carried his gun, and he was not afraid to use it whenever the chance offered. Nothing could have looked more frightful than they, their chests naked, their irregular features daubed with different colored paint, their long black hair dangling about their shoulders, while each rode like a centaur.

A distance of two hundred yards separated the parties, neither of which had made the slightest variation in its course. Our friends were heading directly toward the building and did not swerve to the right or left. To have done so would have shown fear, and brought the redskins down upon them like a cyclone.

One of two things was inevitable, and that within the space of a few seconds: the Apaches or white men must turn to one side, or there would be a fierce fight. Eph Bozeman and his comrades were resolved to keep on until the noses of their ponies should touch. What was the purpose of the red men must appear immediately.

The break came from an unexpected source. Belden Rickard and Harman Slidham had not forgotten the parting words of the trapper, and were on the watch at the upper front windows. The rapidly increasing light showed the four horsemen coming down the slope, and they saw the Apaches set out to meet them. Matters were on the eve of explosion when Rickard took deliberate sight from his window and fired at the warriors. The shot was a long one, but so accurately aimed that a dusky horseman, with a rasping screech, rolled off his pony, the animal breaking into a gallop, circling away from the others, and, facing toward the building, whinneying with fright and dashing aimlessly hither and thither in a panic.

The other Apaches acted as if the report of the gun was the signal for them to break apart, for they did so with a suddenness that could not have been surpassed had a bombshell burst beneath them.

Several turned to the right and others to the left, while one, as if he absolutely feared nothing, headed his black pony directly at

Bozeman and thundered forward on a dead run.

The miscreant was actually charging the whole party.

He emitted a terrifying whoop, leaning almost on his horse's ears, as he brought his rifle round in front to fire, but a master hand at that business had not taken his eye from him since he started on his daring ride. The raising of the gun and the aiming and firing seemed to take place all together, and in the twinkling of an eye.

"Thar's one fool less," was the quiet remark of Eph as he lowered his piece; "now, boys, grab ground."

His pony was stretching away at headlong speed for the building, the others imitating him so quickly that the four continued in a bunch. "Keep it up," he added, firing again at their assailants.

Strubell and Lattin discharged their pieces as often as they could take any sort of aim, but the conditions were against accuracy, and there was no evidence that they did any execution.

The Apaches had branched off to the right and left, and kept popping away, with no more success than the white men. They held the marksmanship of the others in such fear that they gave much effort to screening their bodies, by flinging themselves over the sides of their animals and firing from under the neck or directly over it, where little could be seen of the riders except their glaring eyes and their hair, looking as if they were a part of the mane of their ponies, or the black eyes flashed for a moment in front of the breast of the galloping steeds.

It cannot be said that Herbert Watrous felt pleasant when he heard the bullets singing about his ears, and knew that more than one was aimed at him. He did not attempt to reply, but gave his whole attention to urging Jill to his utmost. The building was only a short way off, and the briefest kind of a respite insured safety.

Fortunately his steed was fully the equal of the others in fleetness and did not fall behind. Had it done so he would not have been left by his friends, for all were governed by that devotion which belongs to the highest form of chivalry. There was not one who would not have protected the youth with his life.

Suddenly the broad door at the front of the adobe building was drawn inward. Rickard and Slidham had hurried down to make sure no delay took place at this critical moment.

Herbert Watrous was leaning forward, with his eyes fixed on the avenue to safety, when he felt Jill shudder under the saddle, as if with a sudden chill. He veered to one side, throwing his nose against the shoulder of the trapper's pony, and staggered uncertainly in the hopeless effort to recover himself, but, unable to do so, plunged forward on his knees and rolled over on his side, gasping his last breath.

"*The building was only a short way off.*"

Page 335.

CHAPTER XXXVIII.

CONCLUSION.

THE thrusting of the mortally wounded pony's nose against the shoulder of the trapper's horse warned both him and Herbert Watrous of what was coming. The latter slipped his feet from the stirrups, and was in the act of leaping to the ground, to attempt to run the short distance to the entrance of the mission building, when the broad right hand of Eph Bozeman slapped him in the broad of the back, clutched his coat, and with one powerful wrench he swung him out of the saddle sinking beneath him, and lifting him over in front of himself on his own steed.

There was not the slightest slackening of speed on the part of the doubly laden animal, who not only held his own, but headed the procession as it dashed through the door, followed by the other two, amid a storm of bullets, as Rickard and Slidham slammed the door shut and fastened it in place.

The whole party was safe, without a scratch, and with only the loss of a single animal.

They could hardly believe their good fortune, until their panting steeds were brought to a halt and the riders slipped to the ground.

Then followed a general handshaking, and it would have been hard to believe that anything like enmity had existed between the men who showed such genuine pleasure at the escape of the little company from the Apaches. But a common danger draws people together, and Rickard and Slidham forgot that but a short time ago they had agreed to return a youth to these same visitors for a certain ransom.

The first thing done after a general exchange of congratulations was on the part of the new arrivals. They made haste to the spring of cool, refreshing water, where they quaffed their fill, their ponies doing the same.

Rickard had made preparations for their coming. From his storehouse of meal and meat he had prepared a nourishing and abundant meal for all. Since there was no grass within the building, the horses were fed with the grain, of which there was sufficient to, last several weeks by the exercise of frugality.

The animals having been attended to and the hunger and thirst of the guests being satisfied, the company gathered in the small room where Eph Bozeman had held his interview of the night before. They crowded the place, but all found seats, and they conversed as freely as if they had been friends for years.

"I made a bad break," said Rickard, with a laugh; "you'll admit that I worked that plan pretty well, but I didn't count on the boy giving me the slip at the last minute."

"Where do you suppose he has gone?" asked Strubell, who did most of the talking for his side, the others listening attentively to every word that was spoken.

"He must have been on the watch when Eph come in; we were all three in this room, talking the matter over, when he slipped out with his pony and has gone, who can say where?"

"It doesn't look as if the Apaches had caught him."

"No; I thought they might have done so, but there would have been an outcry if that took place. We wouldn't have heard the sound of his horse as he rode off, but he would have used his rifle and pistol before allowing himself to be taken, and we must have heard them. He was the pluckiest fellow I ever saw."

"That's so," added Herbert; "Nick Ribsam was a brave boy; he gave me the biggest trouncing I ever had when he wasn't more than half my size, and there's no Indian that can down him without having the worst fight of his life."

"What I don't understand," continued Strubell, "is why he should wait until everything was in the best shape for him, and then slip off and knock our plan endways."

"Didn't he have any chance of gettin' away when you was on the road here?" inquired Lattin.

"Well, we watched pretty close, for we knew what he was thinking of; Harman and

I were never asleep at the same time, and we didn't let him have his gun or pistol while on the road."

Herbert's heart burned with indignation at these words, but he kept silent. He knew now why Nick had remained passive so long. He was too wise to dash away from his captors and ride out on the open prairie, exposed to innumerable dangers, without a weapon at command. Had he been allowed to retain them he would have made things lively for Bell Rickard.

Rickard stated further that they had no field glass at command, like their pursuers, so that they never caught sight of them, though well convinced they were on their trail. Consequently Nick had not the incentive that would have been his had he felt any assurance of meeting his friends if he fled eastward.

"When we arrived here," continued the horse thief, "and we knew the Apaches were close outside, why, we let him have his weapons, for it looked as if he might be able to help us against the redskins."

"Of course when he saw Eph come through

the door and join you in this room," said Strubell, "he had no idea that he came from us; if he had he would have acted differently——"

"No, he wouldn't either; you don't know what you're talkin' 'bout."

It was the old trapper who uttered this exclamation, after he had held his peace for several minutes. All looked at him wonderingly, for it was not clear what he meant by his abrupt remark. His little eyes shone with a peculiar light, and could his mouth have been seen, a singular smile would have been observed playing around it.

"Boys," added Eph, straightening up on his seat as he saw every gaze fixed upon him, "shall I tell you something?"

The expression of general interest convinced him that no one could be heard with greater pleasure.

"Last night, after passin' out the door, a quar idea got into my head. Instead of startin' on a run to get back to you folks, I stooped down and passed my hands over the ground all round the door. And what do you s'pose I found? Why, thar war the prints of several horses goin' in, *but thar warn't a single one comin' out!*"

He paused a moment for this astounding announcement to produce its effect. Strubell was the first to catch its full meaning.

"Are you sure of that?" he asked.

"As sure as I'm sittin' here this minute. What does it mean, tharfore and consequently? Why, that that younker came in with Bell and Harman, but that he *haint gone out, which the same means that he's inside of this buildin' and aint fifty feet off this very minute*, and if thar's anyone here that don't b'lieve me, all he's got to do is to look through that door yonder and tell me whether he don't see the grinnin' younker standin' thar this very minute."

It so happened that as Eph sat he faced the opening of the little room, and, since every eye was fixed on him, their backs were turned in the other direction. All wheeled like a flash and saw Nick Ribsam in the act of entering the apartment, his honest face expanded into one broad smile, while his hand was extended to greet his old acquaintances.

Herbert Watrous stared with open mouth, unable to believe it was not a dream, until his hand was clasped by that of the best friend he had, outside of his own folks, in the world. Then he saw that it was reality, and greeted the good fellow with a delight which touched even the hearts of Bell Rickard and Harman Slidham.

Enough has been hinted about Nick Ribsam to give the reader a general idea of his experience from the night he was made prisoner by the horse thieves and carried westward into New Mexico. Herbert was correct in his surmise as to why he made no effort to escape while on the long journey. With no fire-arms at command, with no knowledge of where his friends were, and believing that his captors were only manœuvring for a ransom, he would have disproved all faith in his good sense had he seized any one of the several occasions for parting company with those whom he despised.

He had no suspicion of the business which brought Eph Bozeman to the building, else he would not have played the little deception he did on his captors; but when requested to betake himself to some other part of the structure during the interview, he obeyed, passing into the room which adjoined the one where the ponies had been placed.

Here he struck a match that he might investigate his surroundings. The first thing that caught his attention was a door, which he did not notice until he was at the further end of the apartment, and then he would not have observed it had not his gaze struck it in a peculiar manner.

A brief examination showed that it was intended by the parties who built the mission house as a secret storehouse or retreat in a last emergency. It was so ingeniously constructed that the space occupied was cut off from three other apartments, and the missing portion was not likely to be noticed unless suspicion happened to be turned that way.

The room was long and narrow, and there was space at one end for a horse, ventilation being secured by means of several slits that were cleverly concealed from view. Of course it would not have required a close search for anyone to discover it from the outside, but that search was not made.

The moment Nick stumbled upon the retreat, the idea of a trick came to him. He led Jack into the space, slipped out and unfastened the door to give the impression that he had passed through it, and then returned and ensconced himself within.

The reflection came to him that he had done an exceedingly risky thing in leaving the door unfastened, but he reasoned that he would soon be missed and the open avenue discovered. Then, too, what band of Apaches, or white persons for that matter, would dream of such a piece of negligence on the part of three persons who knew of their danger?

While debating the matter with himself, and when he was on the point of going out to secure the door again, he fell asleep and did not open his eyes until after the arrival of his friends. The reports of the rifles were so dulled by the intervening walls that they had not disturbed him at all.

Eph Bozeman was convinced of the presence of the youth within the building on his failure to find any hoof prints leading outward from the door. He deemed it best to say nothing of this to his companions, since he wanted to give them a surprise, and he did it beyond question.

What pleased the old trapper was the certainty that Bell Rickard, after all, must lose the thousand dollars, for under the circumstances he had no legal claim to it, inasmuch as Nick had escaped from his custody, and he confessed himself unable to perform his part of the contract.

Our friends were one horse short, and the loss was a severe one. It was decided to stay where they were until the Apaches grew tired of the siege, and communication could be opened with other parties. Jim-John and his companion were supposed to be making their way toward the same destination with the pack horses, one of which could be turned to account in case nothing better presented itself.

But at this interesting juncture Bell Rickard, of all others, solved the difficulty in an unexpected manner. He insisted that he had come by his own horse fairly, and he asked the privilege of furnishing it to Herbert Watrous. He said he would wait where he was until the arrival of Jim-John and Brindage, and accept one of the pack horses in exchange. This was finally agreed to, and the transaction was probably the first honest one of the kind in which the fellow had taken part in a long time.

On the second day all signs of the Apaches disappeared. They had carried off the bodies of those who had fallen, and sought more inviting fields for their cruel work.

Instead of pushing on to California, as Nick and Herbert originally intended, they decided to return to San Antonio with Strubell and Lattin. Herbert had fully recovered his health, and, to tell the truth, both boys were homesick. They felt there was no place like their own homes, and the society of their loved ones. They had been granted that which led them across Texas, and why go further?

It is not necessary to give the incidents of their return to the quaint old town of San Antonio, although the journey was marked by many interesting incidents. They arrived there without serious mishap, and, parting company with the Texans and the old trapper, who was liberally rewarded for his services, Nick, just one week later, clasped his father, mother, and sister Nellie in his arms. Herbert stayed a day with him, and then hastened to his home in New York City, where it need not be said he was welcomed with gratitude and affection.

And here the history of Nick Ribsam and Herbert Watrous properly ends. That they will be the same warm, trustful, loving friends through life need not be said, and the good seed sown by the honest young Pennsylvanian in the heart of his city associate will spring up and bear a blessed fruit, the full degree of which can never be known until they enter upon the life to come.

THE END.

www.ingramcontent.com/pod-product-compliance
Lightning Source LLC
Chambersburg PA
CBHW020230240426
43672CB00006B/478